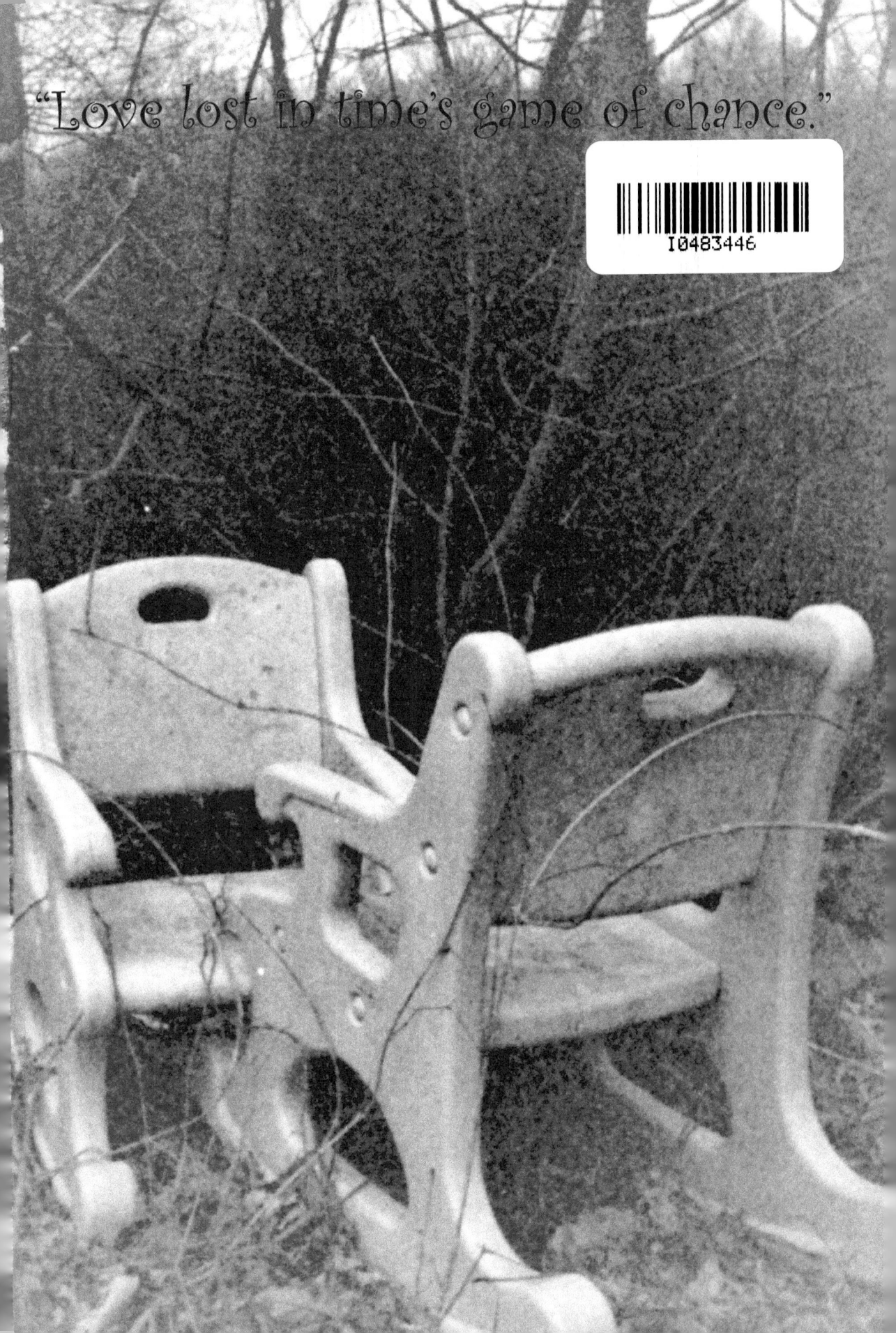

"Love lost in time's game of chance."

Cover, Front, Back and Back-Page Quotes by
Genesis Breyer P-Orridge.

Front Cover Photo: Kieran Canter and Cinzia Monreale
in Joe D'Amato's *Buio Omega*

A Special Thanks to all of my contributors and
Amy Pangburn-Martin.

This issue is dedicated to Vicki.

JEREMY R. RICHEY
220 TUPELO TRAIL 1607
FRANKFORT, KY 40601
VOLUME 2/JUNE, 2019/FIRST PRINTING
NOSTALGIAKINKY.COM

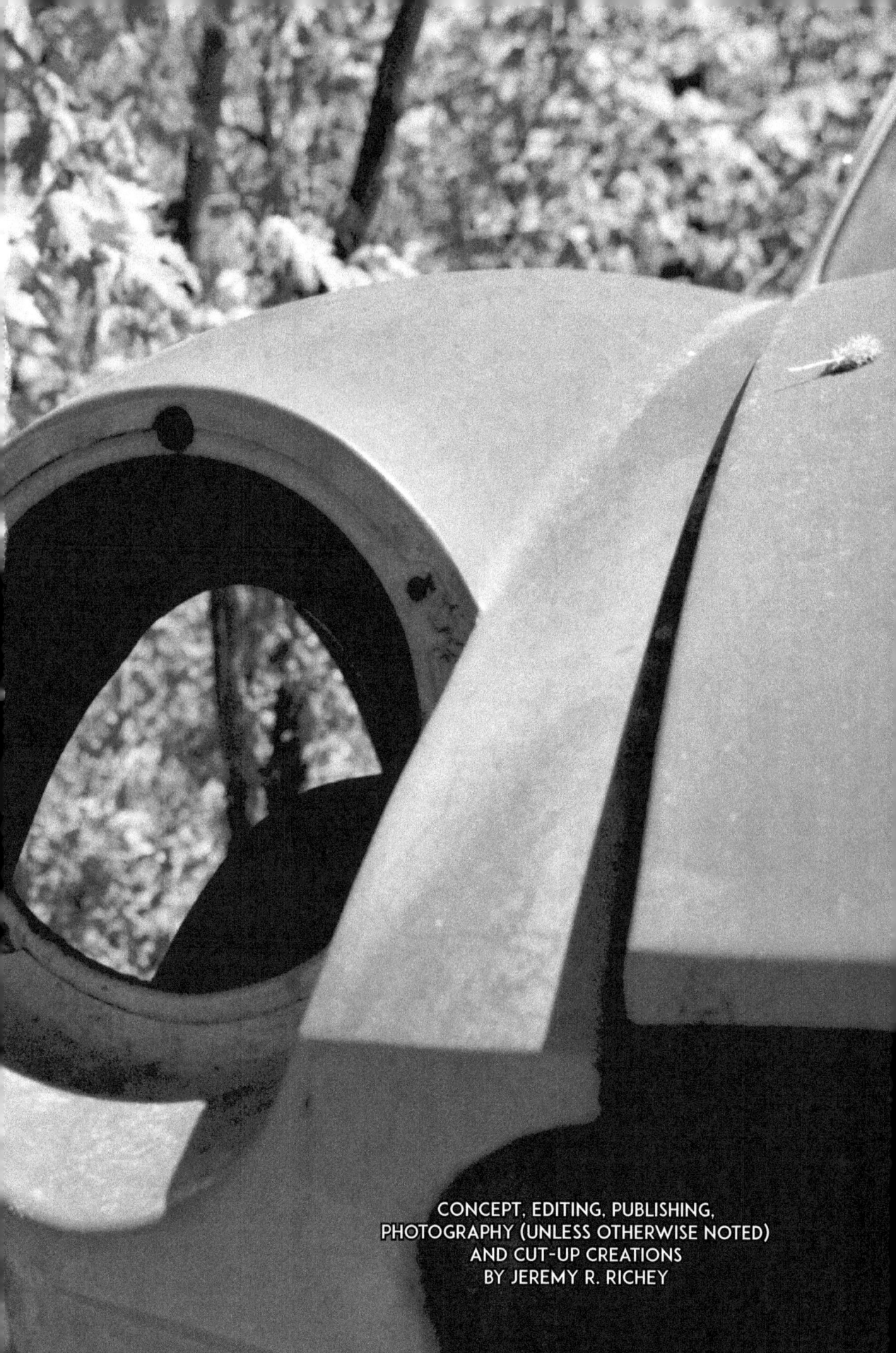

CONCEPT, EDITING, PUBLISHING,
PHOTOGRAPHY (UNLESS OTHERWISE NOTED)
AND CUT-UP CREATIONS
BY JEREMY R. RICHEY

THIS VOLUME OF
SOLEDAD
WAS COMPILED
IN THE SPRING OF 2019
FOR THE SUMMER OF 1989.

IT CONTAINS:

INTERVIEWS WITH
JUSTIN COFFEE,
SAMM DEIGHAN
AND PAUL JOHNSON

FICTION BY LES BOHEM,
MICHAEL A. GONZALES
AND ROBERT MONELL

AN ESSAY BY TARA HANKS

POETRY BY EMILY CLARE BRYANT
AND RORY DEMAIO

A BOOK EXCERPT BY MARCELLINE BLOCK

L★F FILM BUIO ΩMEGA

VIETATO AI MINORI DI 18 ANNI

© FORNI VIDEOCENTER DI
FORNI LAMBERTO
Corso Italia, 126 - 40017 S. Giovanni Persiceto (BO
Tel. 051/82.12.06

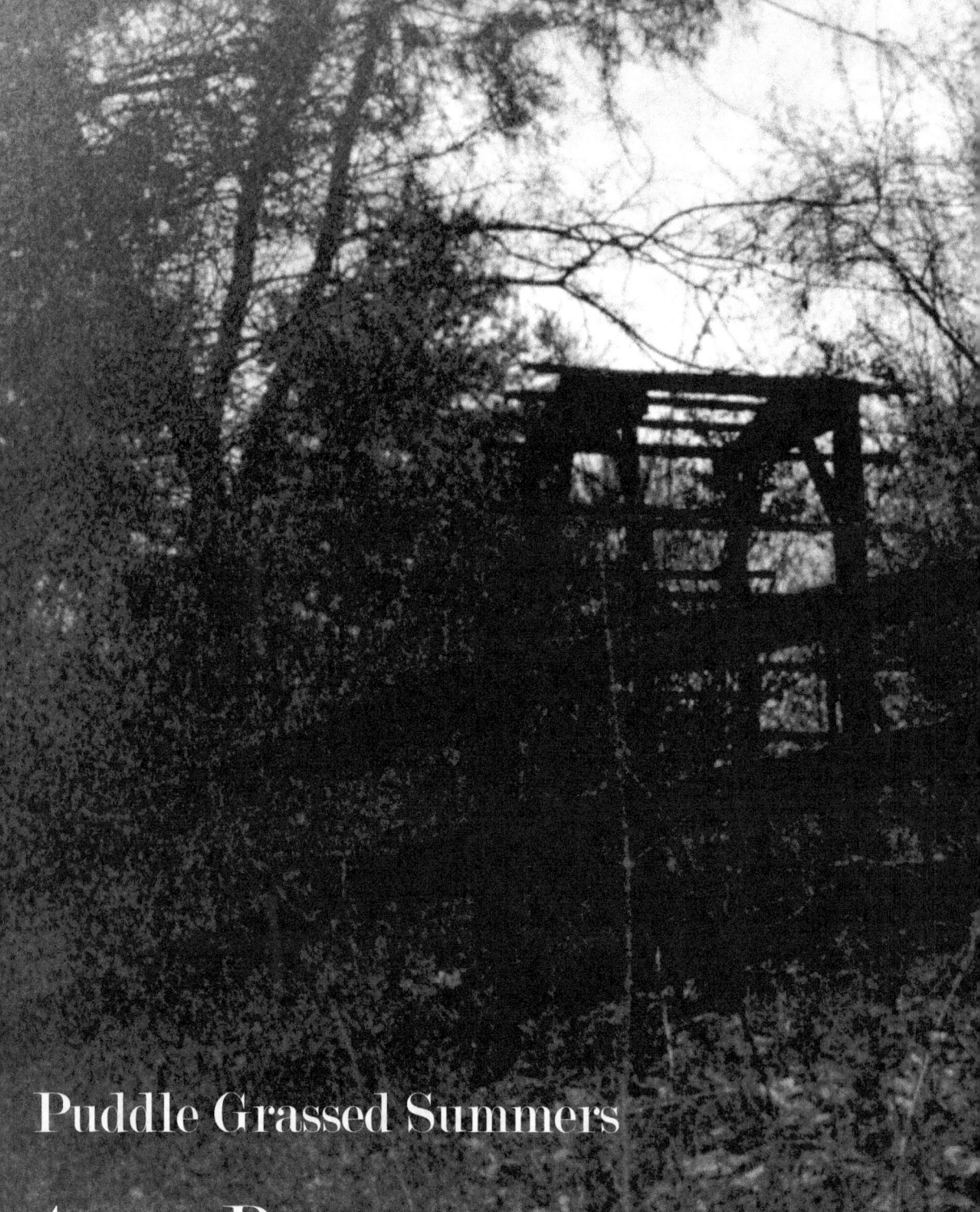

Puddle Grassed Summers

4 new Poems
by Emily Clare Bryant

Photos by Jeremy R Richey (Except portrait of Emily)

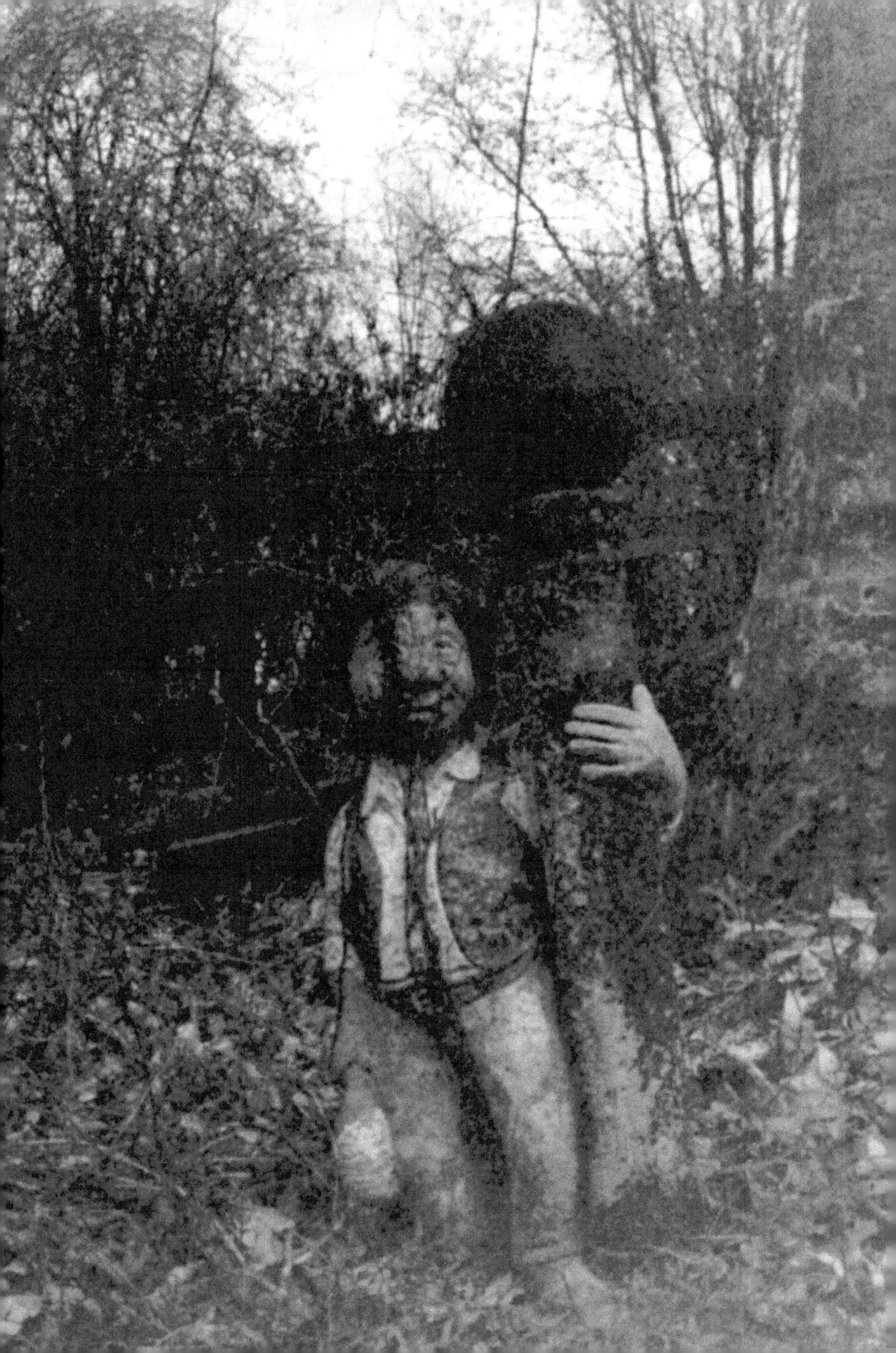

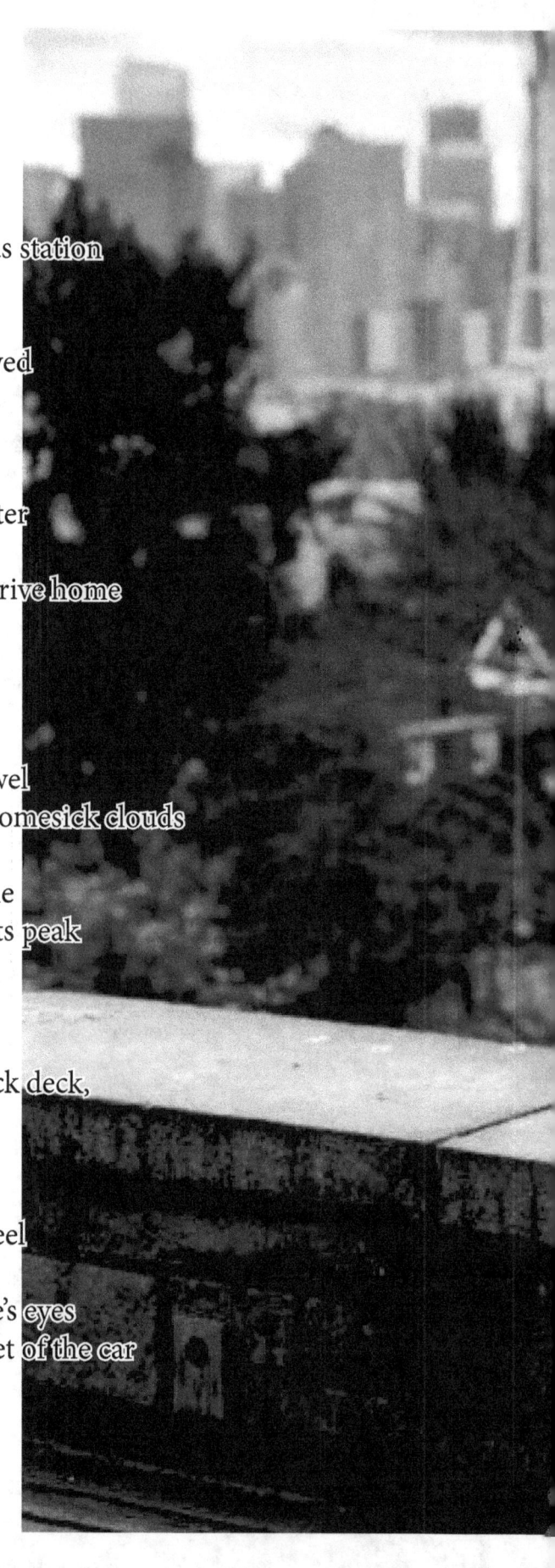

On Black Box Wine

we chug black box merlot from the gas station
under dying purple lipped sun
our big toes crying
grabbing onto the firm grip of borrowed
Seattle Sand, and we wonder
where will we be in ten years?
our sides mesh
they dance alongside estranged laughter
from high school locals,
the friend groups not quite ready to drive home
and there's a softness in the bay
one that ripples just enough
so that its tips remind us
that it's not quite a painting after all
Jessica falls back on our makeshift towel
let's her fingers draw a map into her homesick clouds
where will we be in two years?
my merlot is sticky, salt on soggy ankle
the volleyball game to our right is at its peak
we are dreaming of Kentucky
of puddle grassed summers
and timid pointy dew tips,
our tipsy mothers laughing on the back deck,
pouring stories onto perfect pancakes
the morning after house parties
and the warmth of golden rays
burning fast onto Camry steering wheel
we trudge past mellow trees,
begging for loud breeze, stiff to nature's eyes
tuck our crushed boxes into the pocket of the car
crack down on the gas pedal,
and shuffle back into the city

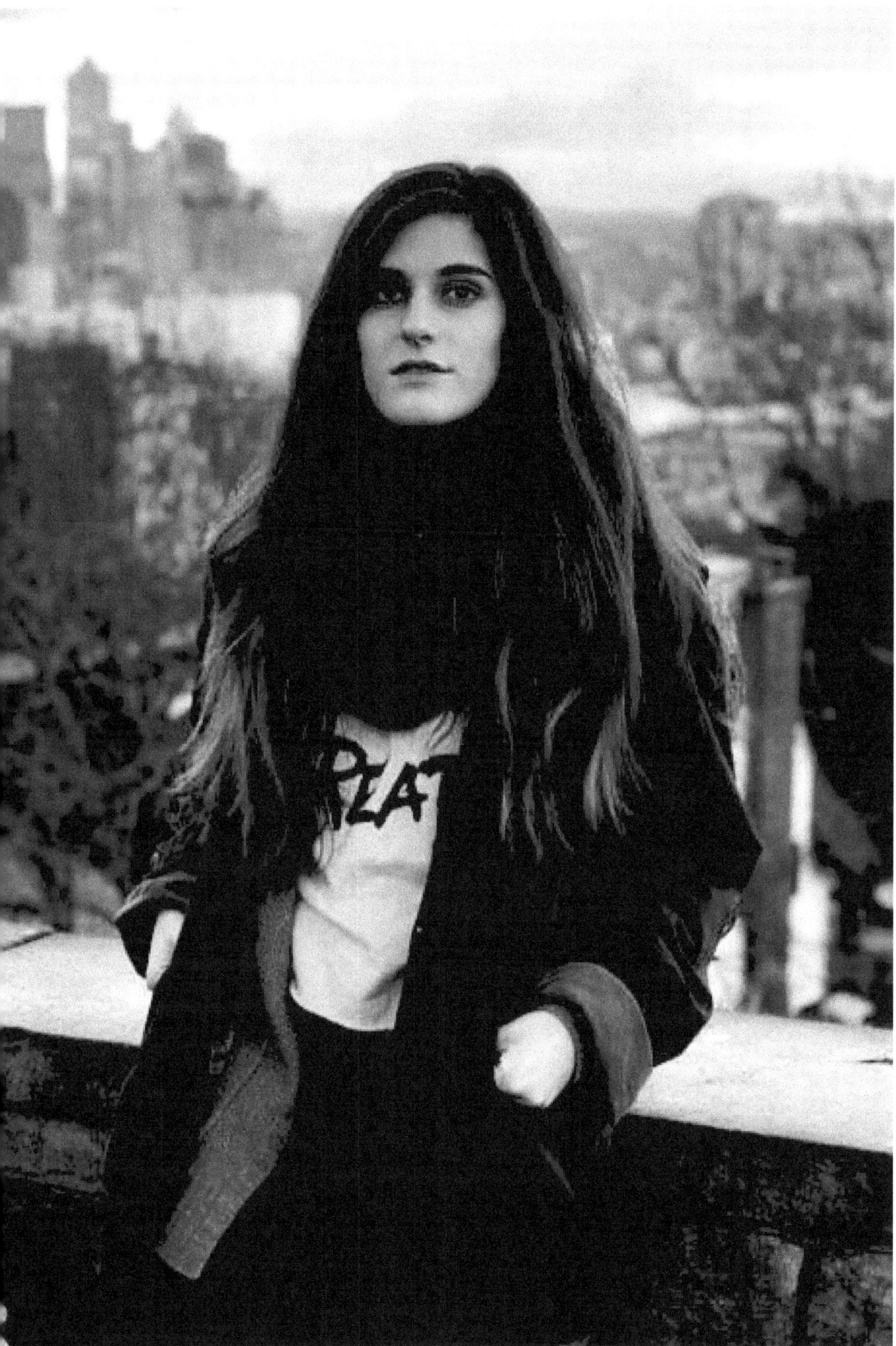

remembering what I've done

there's a baby flame in my belly
one that flicks burnt orange peels onto pillow,
curly fried right into the crinkles of my daisy comforter
it pulls at my neck, makes my internal engine overheat
there's a fire in my belly
one that grows when I feed in its memory
when I nourish its crackles,
the faint blue veins that burst out of my arms
there's a pit right inside me
where waves of guilt are burned into my skin
branded and I stand with lonely
sulk with her until she swallows me whole
there's a baby flame burning
that knows what I've done
it screams for my home,
my love,
and it simmers, and it waits,
rubbing its ash so slowly
against the palms of everyone I touch

when God gave his only son

their sins too heavy for us
so we shrug them off and walk
with lazy heels and rusty ankles
letting our bodies fall flat
tapping away to beat down battles
collecting her bruised memories,
the jaded shadows
that lead the way

their sins too heavy for us
they harden and burrow away,
pop up like ants on our back deck
their pestering presence
a reminder of what these years
for them could have been

there are grudges held by children,
there's forgiveness in his home cooked meal
we tuck time away from sorrow
cradle it in the basket of our arms
and we too, plead to return,
to our full and whimsical colors
from before

Outside my Bedroom Window

there's something in the touch
of silk threaded finger tips
like feathers falling down the spine
gentle, the limpid notes of a song at its death
there's curvature in a voice in its melody
fragile enough to bend at its peak
natural lighting in the kitchen,
the white noise of a Sunday afternoon
it's magical to be touched, so calmly
to be basked in like a neighborhood pool
we are lonely on the concrete
pink freckled undertones, begging to peer out
come new summer day

for there's a brown little bird
one to return to her very own tree
she perches her back tall
and mimics the wind from oncoming traffic
dreams out loud, bold to admit
she misses the twigs
from last year's nest

EMILY CLARE BRYANT IS A KENTUCKY BASED WRITER.
HER FAVORITE POETS ARE BYRON, POE, DICKINSON AND
BLAKE. SHE HAS WANTED TO BE A WRITER SINCE THE THIRD
GRADE AND HER OTHER INTERESTS INCLUDE
PSYCHOLOGY AND SOCIOLOGY.

FOLLOW HER AT
INSTAGRAM AT
SADLUNAGIRL.

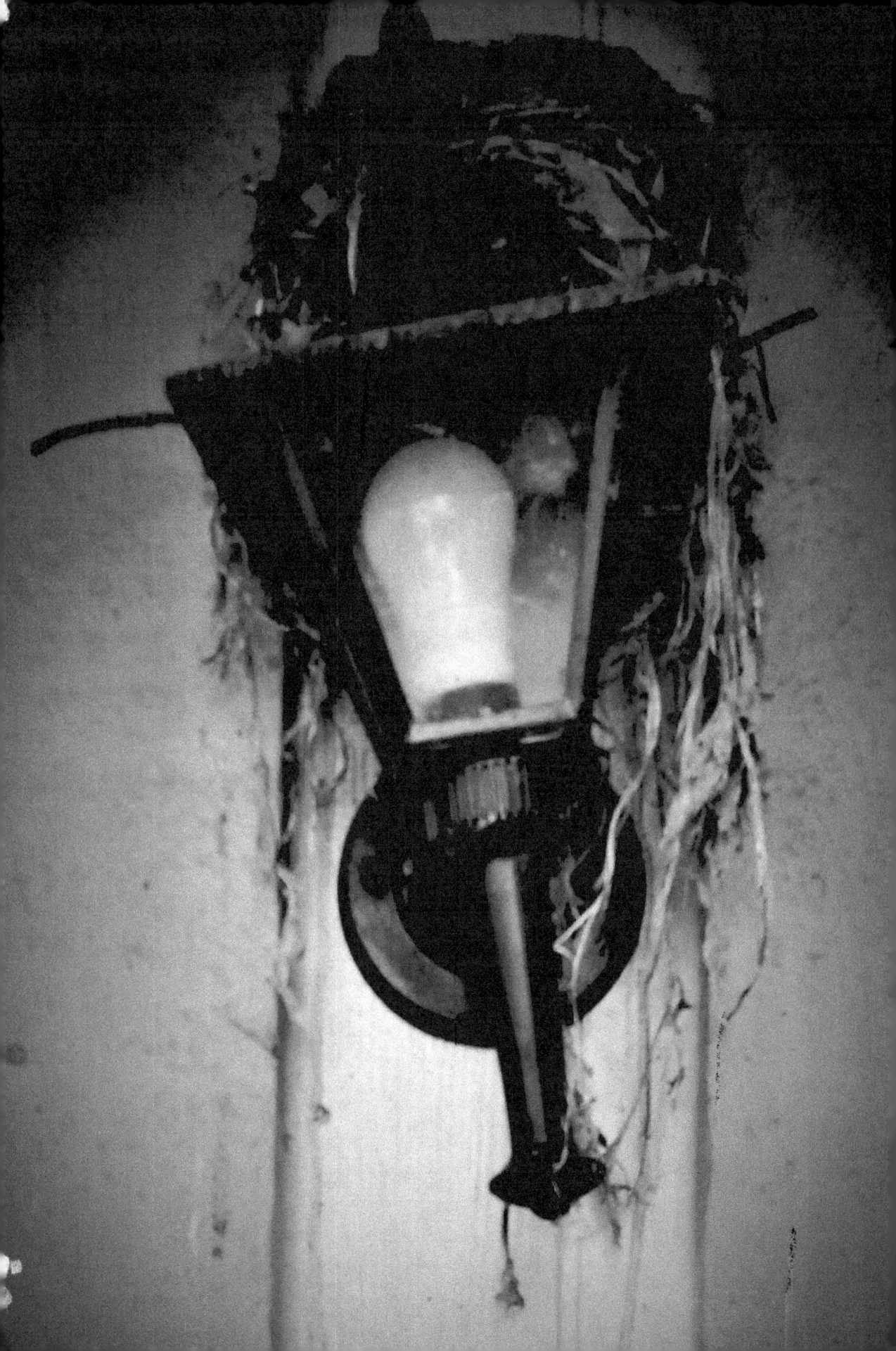

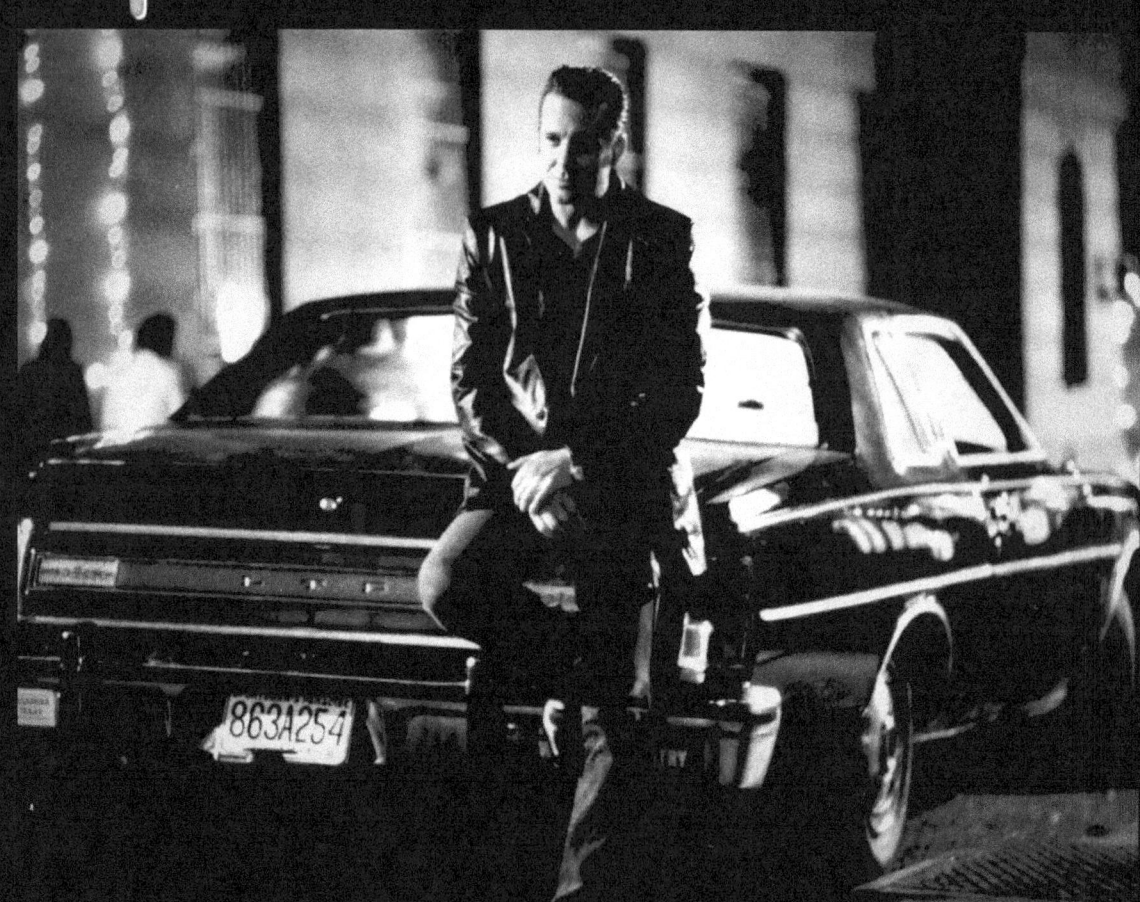

MICKEY ROURKE

JOHNNY
Handsome

"This is a movie in the true tradition of film noir -- which someone who didn't write a dictionary once described as a movie where an ordinary guy indulges the weak side of his character, and hell opens up beneath his feet."

-ROGER EBERT-

MARIO KASSAR and ANDREW VAJNA Present A GUBER-PETERS COMPANY Production A WALTER HILL Film
MICKEY ROURKE JOHNNY HANDSOME Produced in Association with CHARLES ROVEN
ELLEN BARKIN ELIZABETH McGOVERN FOREST WHITAKER SCOTT WILSON LANCE HENRIKSEN
and MORGAN FREEMAN Music By RY COODER Production Designer GENE RUDOLF Director of Photography MATTHEW F. LEONETTI, A.S.C
Executive Producers MARIO KASSAR and ANDREW VAJNA Based upon the novel "The Three Worlds of Johnny Handsome" By JOHN GODEY Screenplay By KEN FRIEDMAN

DOLBY STEREO   Produced By CHARLES ROVEN   Directed By WALTER HILL   A TRI-STAR RELEASE

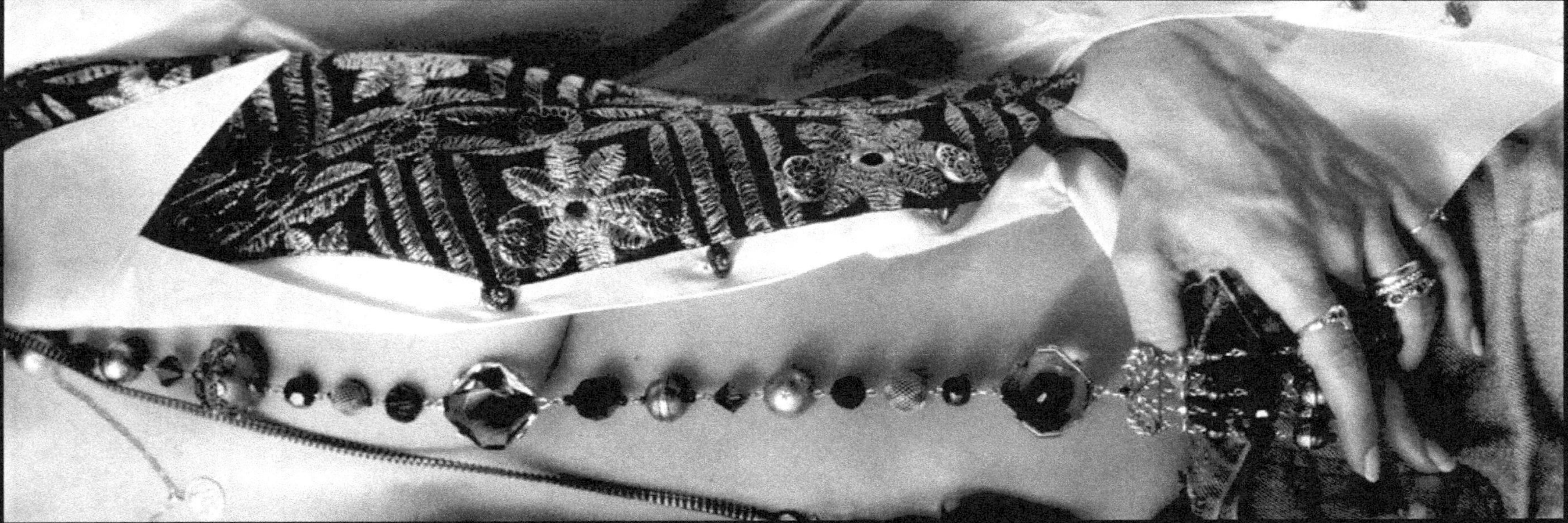

LEAD US INTO TEMPTATION. MADONNA

LIKE A PRAYER
(4/2 / 25844)

HER FIRST STUDIO ALBUM IN THREE YEARS.
RODUCED BY MADONNA AND PATRICK LEONARD

Management:
Freddy DeMann/The DeMann Entertainment Co.

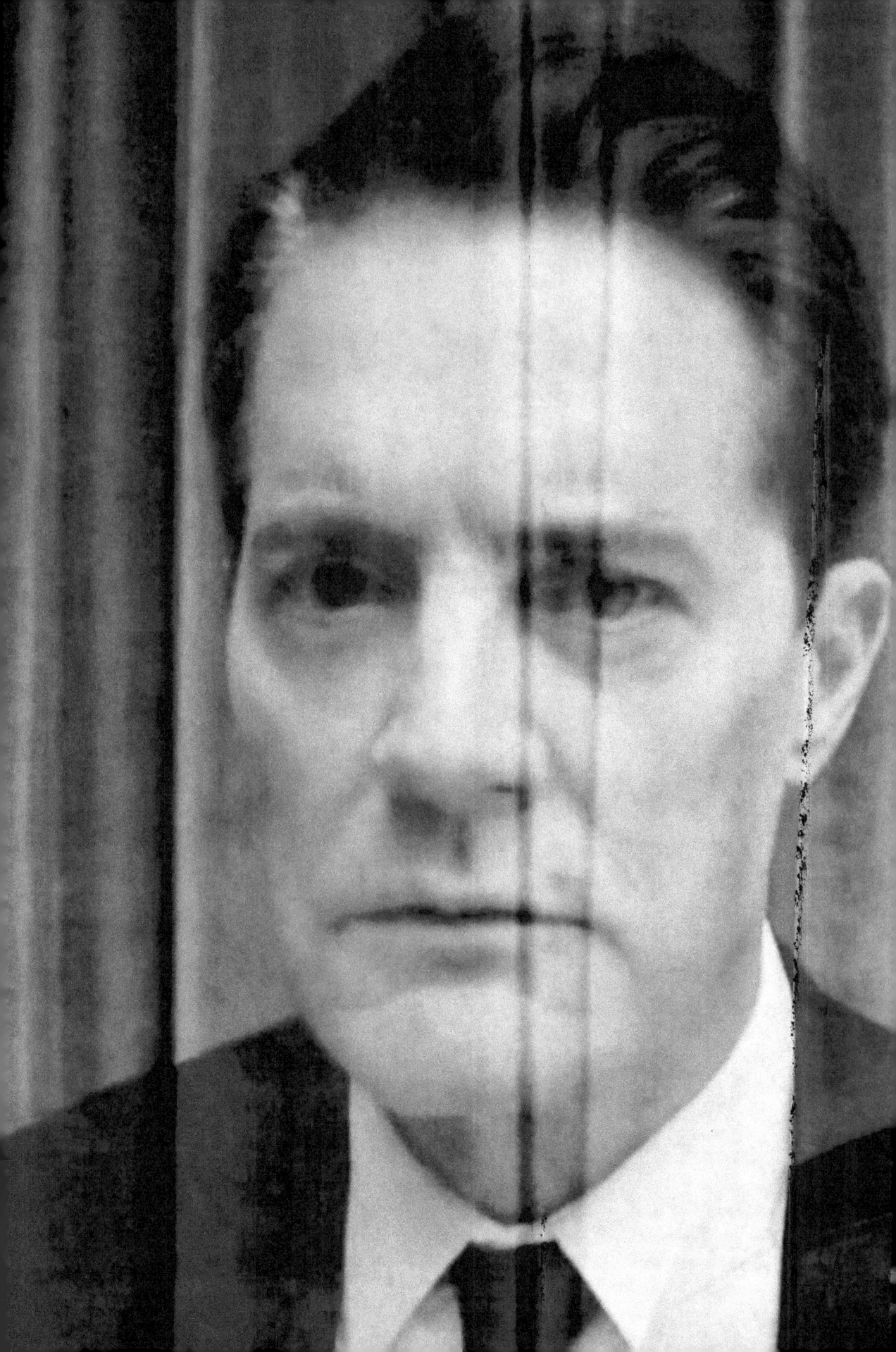

We Are Like The Dreamer:

Visions and Nightmares in Twin Peaks

by

Tara Hanks

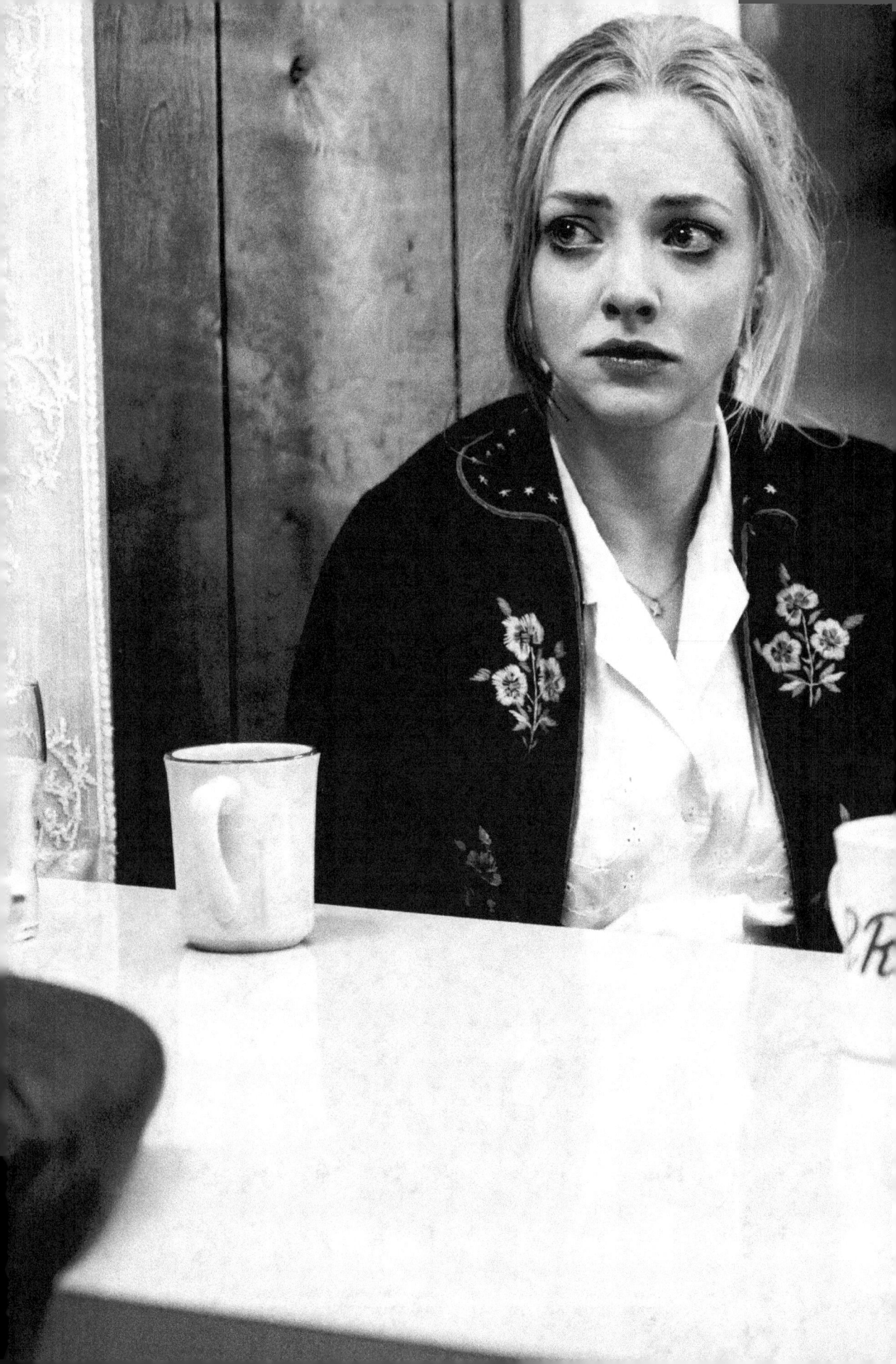

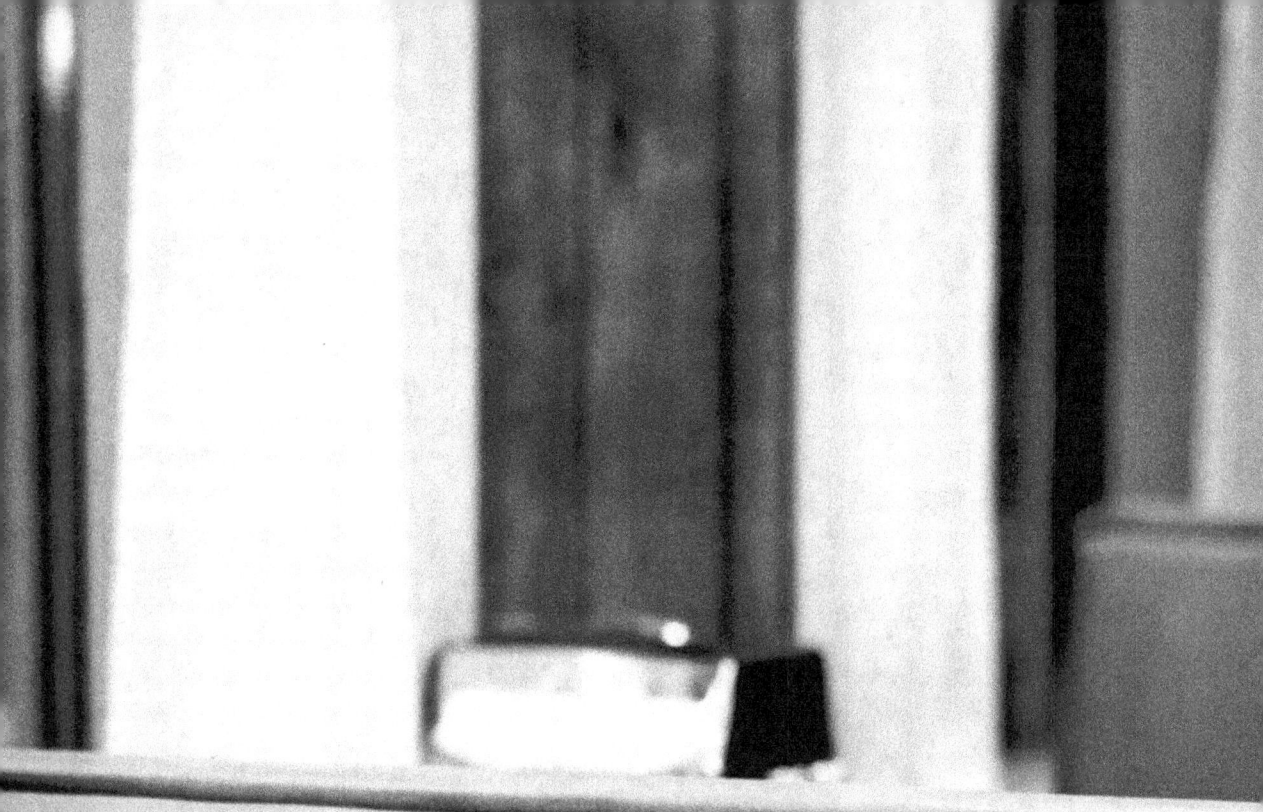

After a twenty-five-year silence, the third season of *Twin Peaks* made its debut in May 2017. In the previous issue of *SOLEDAD*, I looked back at the revival from its inception through the first nine hour-long episodes, which takes us to its midpoint. ▮▮▮ Dale Cooper has ended his long exile and returned in the guise of bumbling insurance salesm▮▮ ▮▮gie Jones. Unfortunately, he is now an un-witting target for Cooper's doppelganger, who is ▮▮▮▮▮rge. In the eighth part of the series, 'Gotta Light?', David Lynch unveiled a creation myth for ▮▮▮▮▮s like Laura Palmer and the demonic BOB, dating back to the atomic bomb tests at New Mex▮▮▮▮▮45. In this essay I will review the next five hours of the show (with occasional reference to M▮▮▮▮'s tie-in books, *The Secret History of Twin Peaks* and *Twin Peaks: The Final Dossier*), while the ▮▮▮▮▮ding installments and critical response will feature in the final part of this trilogy.

The tenth episode opens with a classic American pastoral scene: early morning at the Fat Trout trailer park, and all is quiet. A white trailer, slightly shabby, is enclosed by a small picket fence, and flowers grow within. A beat-up black car, its roof painted red, pulls up outside and Richard Horne calls for Miriam. She answers him from behind the trailer's glass door. From her reflection we gather the wom-an is kindergarten teacher Miriam Sullivan (Sarah Jean Long), last seen tucking into pie and giggling with waitress Heidi at the RR Diner. Long-term employee Shelly watched these two plump, maternal women with a smile, as Miriam gushed: "The kids this year are so *cute!*" She left a generous tip—more than she could afford on a teacher's wage—and Shelly vowed to treat her next time ("She just loves her pies!") But minutes later, Miriam saw Richard (Eamon Farren) driving away from a cross-roads, leaving a dead child in his wake.

Miriam tells Richard she knows what he did, and has sent a letter to the Sheriff's station. He storms into her trailer, and as Miriam screams, we hear the flick of a lighter. She falls silent and he leaves, calling his crony, Deputy Chad Broxtowe, before driving off again. Inside the trailer, a candle has been lit. Miriam lies unconscious beside an open oven door, blood spooling from her head.

Just a few yards away, trailer park manager Carl Rodd is playing 'Red River Valley' on his guitar. It's a traditional song often used in movies, most memorably *The Grapes of Wrath* (1940.) The late Har-ry Dean Stanton plays Carl as a latter-day Jim Casy, and his reedy voice breaks off as a red coffee mug flies out the window of a nearby trailer, smashing the glass. "Fucking nightmare," Carl mutters, echoing his own words after Teresa Banks was murdered in *Twin Peaks: Fire Walk With Me* (1991.) Inside the trailer, junkie Steven Burnett (Caleb Landry Jones) aims a blow at his cowering wife Becky (Amanda Seyfried), whose bakery job isn't bringing in the money to feed his habit. "Don't play the innocent," he snarls. "I know what you did."

In Las Vegas, casino owner Rodney Mitchum (Robert Knepper) is doing his accounts. Like Miriam's, his morning ritual is about to be violently disrupted. Candie (Amy Shiels), one of three pink tutu-clad hostesses never far from the Mitchum brothers' side, enters the room, chasing an elusive fly. Absorbed in her task, she picks up a TV remote and accidentally hits Rodney on the face. She bursts into tears and sits inconsolably by the television, while the other girls tend to a bleeding Rodney. On the flat screen, a weather forecast predicts sunny weather and a newsreader returns to the scene of Dougie Jones' recent confrontation with Ike 'the Spike' Stadtler. The brothers quickly recognize Dougie as their 'Mr. Jackpots': "Turns out our Mr. Jones is actually Mr. Jones," quips Bradley (Jim Belushi), and a guilt-ridden Candie pleads, "Can you ever forgive me?"

Across the city, harried housewife Janey-E (Naomi Watts) has finally made a doctor's appointment for Dougie (Kyle MacLachlan), whose inert demeanor is giving cause for concern. As Dougie strips to the waist, Doctor Ben (John Billingsley) tells Janey-E, "He's lost a lot of weight—in a good way!" This hardly needs saying, as Janey gazes dreamily at her husband's newly-ripped physique. That evening as Dougie feasts on cake, she is still transfixed. Her toes twitching in red pumps, she asks: "Do you find me attractive?" She gets her answer in the bedroom, straddling a grinning Dougie whose arms flap to the side while she cries out his name, waking a startled Sonny Jim. In their blissful post-coital embrace, Dougie parrots her words: "Love you."

At her office in Twin Peaks, Nadine (Wendy Robie) is watching Dr. Amp's latest vlog about Big Pharma, nodding her agreement between sips of her health shake. "Stop distracting yourselves!" thunders the online guru, aka former town shrink Lawrence Jacoby (Russ Tamblyn.) Outside Nadine's office, it's dark and we see curtains drawn back to reveal one of Dr. Amp's golden shovels on a shopfront bearing the legend: *RUN SILENT, RUN DRAPES.*

Daylight, and a lost Jerry Horne (David Patrick Kelly) holds his out-of-charge phone aloft as he wanders through woodland: "You can't fool me," he yells, "I've been here before!" At the Sheriff's station, Deputy Chad (John Pirrucello) chats aimlessly with receptionist Lucy (Kimmy Robertson), but can't resist mocking her happy marriage to Deputy Andy. When the mail van pulls up, she watches from the window and the postman looks on suspiciously while Chad searches for Miriam's letter.

After reading a text from Chad ("DONE"), Richard drives on to his grandmother's home. Last seen crashing into a wall, Richard's autistic uncle Johnny is now strapped to a dining room chair, facing a bizarre toy bear with a lightbulb head set inside a glass ball, repeating the robotic line: "Hello Johnny, how are you today?" When Richard bursts in, a terrified Sylvia Horne (Jan D'Arcy) appears. He demands all her money and she offers up her purse, but he wants to know where the safe is. Johnny (played by stuntman Erik Rondell) tries to break free and falls to the floor. Sylvia tries to comfort her son, while Richard yells: "Why do you have to make something simple so difficult?"

Throughout the scene, Mantovani's 'Charmaine' plays—the same instrumental used in *One Flew Over the Cuckoo's Nest,* Milos Forman's 1975 satire set in a psychiatric hospital. This ultraviolent attack also recalls Stanley Kubrick's *A Clockwork Orange* (1971), with Richard a latter-day Droog. Later, Sylvia will call her estranged husband, Ben Horne (Richard Beymer) at the Great Northern Hotel. "I'm not sending you any more!" he snaps back at her demands for money. With a sigh, Ben gives in to temptation and asks his assistant Beverly (Ashley Judd) to dinner.

In Las Vegas, Mr. Todd (Patrick Fischler) summons Dougie's co-worker, Anthony Sinclair (Tom Sizemore), ordering him to frame on Dougie for the Mitchum brothers' $130 million insurance loss, which was in fact instigated by Anthony and Mr. Todd (himself in hock to crime boss Mr. C.) As Todd tells a fearful Anthony that if he fails to deliver, "you'll have to kill Mr. Jones yourself." The brothers watch Anthony enter the Silver Mustang Casino from the camera room. Candie, Mandie and Sandie lean on the wall, blending in with the shadows. As the brothers tell Candie to fetch Anthony, she twirls a gloved arm. Her earlier remorse has vanished, and she lazily strolls downstairs. The brothers watch her on camera, and both sigh while she stalls Anthony with irrepressible chatter. "Did we ask her to tell her life story?" an exasperated Bradley fumes, but Rodney says with pity: "She's got nowhere to go."

Candie has been regaling Anthony with the same weather forecast she heard on TV that morning. "You have an enemy in Douglas Jones," Anthony tells the brothers, implicating Dougie in the arson attack on another of their casinos. The brothers vow revenge on the erstwhile Mr. Jackpots: "You fuck us once, shame on us.

You fuck us twice, shame on you!"
In the Mayfair Hotel in Buckhorn, South Dakota, Albert Rosenfield (Miguel Ferrer) dines with pathologist Constance Talbot (Jane Adams.) His boss Gordon Cole (played by director David Lynch) and rookie Tammy Preston (Chrysta Bell) peek as the crusty FBI agent chats with his new love. Before the night is out, however, Albert will visit Cole's room. Gordon is sketching a deer, and a giant hand stretched towards it, when he hears the knock. When he answers, a vision of Laura Palmer appears. (She is crying, in a clip from *Fire Walk With Me*.) As the image recedes, Albert walks in and shares a text message intercepted from Diane's phone, tracing it back to a server in Mexico. Tammy arrives with a surveillance photo of Mr. C—Agent Cooper's malign double— in the elevator at the 'glass box building' in New York City.

At the Twin Peaks Sheriff's Station, Deputy Hawk (Michael Horse) receives another call from the 'Log Lady', Margaret Lanterman (played by Catherine Coulson.) The ailing Margaret shares a stream of consciousness, with the last line giving this episode its title:

"Hawk, electricity is humming. You hear
it in the mountains and rivers. You see it
dance among the seas and stars and glowing around the moon. But in these days, the
glow is dying. What will be in the darkness
that remains? ... Now the circle is almost
complete. Watch and listen to the dream
of time and space. It all comes out now,
flowing like a river, that which is and is not.
Hawk, Laura is the one."

We return to the Roadhouse, where Rebekah Del Rio sings 'No Stars'. The song was co-written with David Lynch, and is sung in both English and Spanish. Del Rio made a musical cameo in *Mulholland Drive* (2001.) One of the show's lush mother figures (like the goddess Senorita Dido in Part 8), Rebekah is poured into a dress with the same chevron pattern seen on the floor of the red room. Like Candie and Laura before her, she snakes her arm cryptically.

"My dream is to go
To that place
You know the one
Where it all began
On a starry night..."

This seven-minute performance (backed by Moby on guitar) is a highlight of the series,

and like the Chromatics' 'Shadow', it reveals the Roadhouse as a liminal space.

There's Fire Where You Are Going
Morning again, and two boys are playing catch at the edge of the Fat Trout trailer park when they spot a bloodied, nude woman crawling through the trees. The eldest boy (played by Travis Frost, son of *Twin Peaks* co-creator Mark Frost) tells his brother to fetch mom and stares in disbelief at Miriam Sullivan, who has barely survived Richard's attack. This disturbing incident is based on a boyhood experience of David Lynch, and is a recurring motif in his work (Isabella Rossellini played out a different version of this scene back in 1986, in *Blue Velvet*.) Inside her trailer, a panicked Becky calls her mother at the RR Diner, telling Shelly (Mädchen Amick) that her husband Steven is missing. After hanging up, she screams with rage, and retrieves a gun from under the coach (in an echo of the original series, where her mother tried to protect herself from the abusive Leo Johnson.) When Shelly arrives, Becky grabs her car keys and drives away, not stopping even after Shelly jumps onto the bonnet. Shelly falls to the ground, weeping, and Carl Rodd hails a lift into town. En route, he contacts the Sheriff's Station direct—clearly, Carl has the ear of the local police. "Bobby, she's got a gun!" Shelly cries helplessly.

Meanwhile, Becky pulls up outside an apartment building, runs upstairs and yells for Steven. When no reply comes, she fires at the door. She screams again—"Fuck you, Steven!"—and a neighbour says nobody's there, while Steven hides in the stairwell with Gersten Hayward (Alicia Witt.) Youngest of the three Hayward sisters, Gersten was once a musical prodigy, but is now the only family member remaining in Twin Peaks. At the Sheriff's Station, dispatcher Maggie Brown (Jodee Thelen) fields calls from residents alarmed by the gunfire. In Buckhorn, Gordon Cole and his cohorts follow Bill Hastings (Matthew Lillard) and Detective Dave Macklay (Brent Briscoe) to a vacant lot. "*This* is the place?" Cole looks out on the inauspicious location where Hastings claims to have entered 'the Zone' with girlfriend Ruth. "This is as far as I go," Diane says, watching a scruffy man appear and vanish again across the fence. As Cole and Albert venture forth, a mini-tornado sweeps ash into the sky. Cole walks towards it with arms stretched wide, and has a vision of woodsmen on a staircase. For a moment, he disappears, until Albert pulls him back. They notice a woman's headless corpse, and Albert quips: "Ruth Davenport, I presume?" Outside the lot, Diane sees two shadowy figures enter the car. She nods, as if the woodsmen are familiar to her. (These charred, zombie-like figures were seen stalking the New Mexico desert after the nuclear tests in Part 8.) There is an explosion, and the head of Bill Hastings melts. Diane peers through the window, and as Macklay calls for backup she murmurs, "There's no backup for this."

In the RR Diner that night, Becky sits with Bobby (Dana Ashbrook) and Shelly. "I hate him," she says of Steven. "I want out." But when her parents offer to help, she changes her mind: "He's just going through a bad time." Bobby asks if Steven has ever hit her, and she denies it with exaggerated petulance. While mother and daughter embrace, Bobby gazes at them lovingly. But his happiness is short-lived, as drug dealer Red (Balthazar Getty) knocks on the window and a delighted Shelly runs into the street for a passionate kiss. Bobby's expression is pained, reflecting a bitter irony: his moral redemption has cost him his only true love. When Shelly returns, the group falls silent. Red's appearances always seem to presage disaster: after unnerving Richard with his conjuring tricks, a young boy was killed in a hit-and-run. This will be Red's final scene, leaving another mystery unsolved. Now a gunshot fires into the diner, and Bobby runs outside.

A mother berates her husband for putting a gun in their young son's car-seat. The boy (Elias Parenzini), who wears an army jacket like his dad, could be Sonny-Jim's evil twin; and his scowl suggests this was no accident. An appalled Bobby turns to the car behind, asking the driver (Laura Kenny) to stop honking her horn. The vexed woman explains that they're going home, where an uncle will join them. (In *Twin Peaks*, uncles often codify incest: in the original series, Leland/Bob murdered his niece.) The girl in the back is sick, the woman says. The child (Priya Diane Niehaus) leans forward as if in a trance, vomits greenish slime, and the woman becomes hysterical again.

Inside the Sheriff's Station, Frank Truman (Robert Forster) and Deputy Hawk are studying a map. They are briefly interrupted by the sweet but inexperienced Deputy Jesse Holcomb (James Grixoni), who talks incessantly about his new car, never mentioning the gunshots at the RR. The map is designed by Michael Horse, whose role as Hawk draws upon his Native American heritage. It is, he explains, "very old but always current … *a living thing.*" Hawk points out Blue Pine Mountain, "a sacred site"; a fire symbol, signifying electricity, which can be used for good or bad, depending on intention; and black corn, meaning death, disease, the unnatural. As Frank points out what we recognize as the owl symbol, drawn onto a playing card by Mr. C and shown to Darya immediately before he killed her. "You don't ever want to know about that," Hawk warns Frank. Another call comes in from Margaret, who tells Hawk: "There's fire where you are going."

At the Buckhorn police department, Cole's arm is trembling. "Cat on a hot tin roof," he says, "it's never done this before." In the original series, residents of Twin Peaks experienced the same affliction; as did Teresa Banks before her murder. And more recently, the 'real' Dougie Jones' arm tingled before his return to the red room. Back in the present, Albert watches another 'cat'—the inscrutable Diane, perched on a stool—and notices her trying to read the co-ordinates scribbled on Ruth Davenport's outstretched arm, captured on his cellphone. Tammy brings the coffee, and Dave Macklay endears himself to Diane when he waives the 'no cigarettes' rule: "Smoke 'em if you've got 'em." She drops her guard and mentions the men she saw by the car, but quickly adds, "I could be mistaken." Diane's slip reminds Cole of his own vision: "I saw them," he barks. "Dirty, bearded men in a room!"

In Las Vegas, sprightly Lucky 7 insurance boss Bushnell Mullins (Don Murray) is doing press-ups when Phil Bisby (Josh Fadem) lures Dougie to his office with coffee. "Your investigative work has exposed a ring of organized crime and possible police corruption," Mullins tells a blank-faced Dougie. The Mitchum brothers are not part of it; and by discovering Anthony's collusion, Dougie has righted a wrong. Mullins hands Dougie a $30 million check to cover their damages. They go outside, and Dougie sees the One-Armed Man (Al Strobel) beckoning from the red room. He leads him to Szymon's coffee shop, where Dougie finds a pie. The Mitchum brothers' chauffeur Al (Jay Larson) is waiting in a limousine, and Mullins—reliving his glory days as a prize-fighter—punches the air as Dougie gets in. Al drives past the city limits with Dougie, and we hear Shawn Colvin's leisurely cover of 'Viva Las Vegas.'

The Mitchum brothers have arranged to meet Dougie in the desert, and still believing him responsible for their loss, are planning to kill him. But Bradley had a strange dream, and tells a skeptical Rodney to take off the plaster: the scar on his cheek has miraculously healed. They arrive at a fork in the road to find Dougie holding a white box. Bradley opens it to finds the pie he saw in his dream; after frisking Dougie, he produces the check, and these menacing goons are instantly transformed into Dougie's dearest friends. Grinning from ear to ear, Brad joins Rodney and they hoot in unison: "I *love* this guy!"

When night falls, the brothers are eating pie with Dougie in a restaurant. When the showgirls arrive, the men ask what kept them so long. "There was so much traffic," Candie says dreamily. (Actress Amy Shiels created a backstory for Candie as a past victim of trafficking, rescued by the Mitchum brothers. Seemingly unfamiliar with the ways of the world, has Candie—like Dougie/Cooper—been given a second chance at life?)

'Mrs. Jackpots' (Linda Porter), the bag lady guided by Dougie towards a slot-machine bonanza, approaches the table. Now elegantly dressed, she clutches a white poodle and is accompanied by her son, with whom she has reconciled. "I hope you know what a special person you have with you," she tells the smiling brothers. Turning to Dougie, she whispers tenderly, "I'm so grateful I got a chance to say thank-you again." Dougie is enhancing the lives of everyone he meets; and if their happiness is equated with money, that's a Vegas state of mind. A pianist (Smokey Miles) plays 'Heartbreaking', composed by Angelo Badalamenti, at varying speeds until the credits roll.

Something Happened To Me
At the Mayfair Hotel in Buckhorn, Gordon and Albert are joined by Tammy. They sit around a coffee table, and Albert talks about the history of the Blue Rose Task Force. Since its foundation, the team's ranks have dwindled; with Phillip Jeffries, Chet Desmond and Dale Cooper all missing in action, only two remain. As she sips her red wine, we notice the auburn glint of Tammy's hair. Realizing she's being asked to join them, Tammy agrees without hesitation: "I'm in!" Gordon beams at her fondly, and Badalamenti's 'The Chair' plays.

When Diane arrives, the mood swiftly changes. She slips through red curtains that enclose the group, suggesting her proximity to the red room. When asked to be deputized temporarily, she snaps back: "What's in it for me?" A little money, and maybe the chance to learn what happened to Cooper. With a twisted grin, she makes a peculiar hand gesture and says, "*Let's rock.*" (This was first uttered by Michael J. Anderson—aka the Man From Another Place—in the original series, and scrawled in lipstick on a car window in *Fire Walk With Me*.)

In the first of several short scenes, the waylaid Jerry Horne runs through a meadow, like a stoner parody of Julie Andrews in *The Sound of Music*. In Las Vegas, Dougie and Sonny Jim play catch in the garden. As Sonny Jim throws the ball, Dougie remains immobile and the ball hits him on the head. It's a touching, if silly, father-and-son moment, one of many physical gags performed by Kyle MacLachlan as Dougie. A later scene shows Miriam Sullivan lying bruised and comatose in an ICU—a reminder of Ronette Pulaski's tragic fate after narrowly escaping death with Laura.

In a Twin Peaks supermarket, Sarah Palmer fills her trolley with vodka and tomato juice. At the checkout, she is served by a teenage girl (Zoe McLane), whose long blonde hair evokes Sarah's dead daughter. Behind the girl, a packet of 'Turkey Jerky' is on sale. Sarah becomes disturbed by this unnatural product. (In *Fire Walk With Me*, Laura tells James Hurley, "I'm gone, long gone, like a turkey in the corn." With her psychic insight, has Sarah accessed a buried memory?)

As the bemused girl tries to calm her, Sarah becomes hysterical. "Were you there when they came?" she asks the girl. "Your room seems different. Men are coming … *Something happened to me!*" She tries to pull herself together, muttering, "Sarah, stop doing this. Leave this place—get the car-keys …" Sarah hurries out, leaving her shopping behind. As the girl puzzles over the incident, a bag-boy (Johnny Ochsner) offers to deliver it: he knows where Mrs. Palmer lives.

At the Fat Trout trailer park, Carl Rodd talks with Kriscol (Bill O'Dell), a portly, middle-aged tenant who has fallen on hard times, and is making ends meet by doing odd jobs for neighbours and selling blood at the hospital. Carl gives him $50, and tells him not to pay his rent this month: "I don't like people selling blood to eat," he tells Kriscol, adding, "You've given enough already."

Having heard about Sarah's odd behavior, Hawk visits the Palmer home. Her groceries have been delivered, and she's already downed a few Bloody Marys. Her eyes are glazed, but her manner is razor-sharp. "I just don't know what came over me," she cuts in sarcastically, as the old ceiling fan whirs at the top of the stairs. "Is there somebody in the house?" Hawk asks, amid the sound of clinking glass. "No, just something in the kitchen," she retorts. Eying him fiercely, she adds, "It's a goddamn bad story, isn't it, Hawk?"

In the Mayfair Hotel bar, Diane carefully removes an olive from her Martini, as if like Sarah, she disdains all nourishment. A text message arrives: "LAS VEGAS?" Her body trembles, but she quickly texts back: "THEY HAVEN'T ASKED YET." Having intercepted this latest exchange, Albert knocks on Cole's door. Gordon is entertaining a beautiful French woman in a red dress (played by a former Bond bad girl, Bérénice Marlohe.) Albert claims urgent business, but the lady is in no hurry. After Gordon promises to meet her in the bar, she performs a series of exaggerated gestures: lifting a shapely leg to reveal her 'Fetish' shoes (red with a black heel, designed by Lynch with Christian Louboutin); taking out a compact mirror and redoing her lipstick; sipping her wine; and blowing Gordon a kiss.

This sequence is reminiscent of a scene in *Fire Walk With Me* where Gordon introduces his 'mother's sister's girl,' redhead Lil, who performs a strange dance. But whereas Lil's actions were partly decoded by Cole, the French woman remains ambiguous. "She's here visiting a friend of her mother's whose daughter has gone missing," he tells Albert, who is more interested in discussing Diane's message. "Albert, sometimes I really worry about you," Gordon says gently; and this line is even sadder in retrospect, as actor Miguel Ferrer would pass away before the show aired.

Sheriff Frank Truman visits Ben at the Great Northern Hotel, and tells him that his nephew, Richard Horne, is responsible for the car accident which killed a young boy. He also mentions another of Richard's victims, Miriam, whose teacher's salary will not cover the operation she needs. Ben sighs, and promises to cover her bills. "That boy was never right," he says. "Richard never had a father." Once a ruthless, philandering businessman, Ben now seems resigned to atoning for not only his own past misdeeds, but also the Horne family's collective sins. As Frank prepares to leave, Ben remembers that the old-fashioned key to Cooper's room arrived in the mail that day (found in Las Vegas by Dougie's call-girl pal, Jade), and Frank agrees to pass it on to his sick brother Harry, former Sheriff and once close to Cooper. After Frank's departure, Beverly joins Ben and he reminisces about a bike his father once gave him.

Chantal (Jennifer Jason Leigh) and Hutch (Tim Roth), the husband-and-wife assassins employed by Mr. C, wait in a van outside the home of Dwight Murphy (James Morrison), Warden of Yankton Prison, where their boss was recently detained. Chantal complains that she is bored, and hungry: "We don't have time for torture, baby," Hutch replies. A young boy (Luke Judy) runs out of the house as Murphy's car pulls up, but by the time he reaches his dad, Hutch has shot him dead. "Next stop Wendy's!" he tells Chantal, setting down his gun as they drive off in search of fast food, indifferent to the trauma inflicted on a helpless child.

On White Tail Peak—"the American Hindu Kush"—Dr. Amp is "doing the vamp for liberty." As the U.S. Army Band's 'Stars and Stripes Forever' plays faintly, he talks of being "sold down the river to die." In her downtown office, regular viewer Nadine seems upbeat: "It's working for me, Dr. Amp," she purrs. We leave the good doctor warning us that "the ninth circle of Hell will welcome you," and cut to Audrey Horne (Sherilyn Fenn) standing by a fire. In her first appearance this season, Audrey wants to go to the Roadhouse and look for a man named Billy, who is missing. Her diminutive husband, Charlie (Clark Middleton) sits at a desk, preoccupied with accounts and deadlines.

"Why do you put me down for doing my allotted duty?" Charlie whines, and it seems their marriage is part of this obligation. He wants her to sign some papers, but she thinks they're "fishy." "You'd go back on a contract?" he asks. Audrey tells him she's in love with Billy. "I saw Billy in my dream last night and he was bleeding from the nose and mouth," she says. "And dreams sometimes hearken a truth …" When Charlie dismisses her concerns, she mocks him for presuming to know better. "I don't have a crystal ball," he protests, though there is one right on his desk.

Audrey puts on a silky red jacket, a more tailored affair than the silk bowling jackets favoured by the younger women of Twin Peaks. There are "thousands of square miles of woods" between them and the Roadhouse, Charlie complains; an exaggeration, perhaps, but his comment suggests they are on the far side of Ghostwood Forest. Charlie agrees to call Tina, whom Audrey loathes; but she may know something about Billy. The conversation seems ominous—"Unbelievable what you're telling me," Charlie tells Tina—but after hanging up, he is too stunned to speak. Audrey's frustration mounts: "You're not going to tell me?" Chromatics give their second Roadhouse performance, playing the instrumental 'Saturday' while two beautiful women, Abbie (Elizabeth Anweis) and Natalie (Ana de Reguera) gossip in the same red booth where so many dialogues—and fights—take place. They're looking for Angela, who might be with Clark, who's also seeing Mary. Mary is off her meds, and there's no telling how she'll react if she finds out about Angela. A bedraggled man named 'Trick' (Scott Coffey) arrives, talking of being run off the road. While Trick goes to the bar, Abbie asks if he's still under house arrest, and a giggly Natalie tells her his sentence is up. (The convoluted relationships of these obscure characters recall the improbable plotlines of *Invitation to Love*, the night-time drama watched by local residents in the original series.)

It's Like Ghostwood In Here

"A wrong has been made right and the sun is shining bright." Still celebrating, Dougie and the Mitchum brothers dance in a conga line through the offices of Lucky 7 Insurance, and as a rinky-dink electronica tune plays, Anthony hides under his desk. He calls Mr. Todd, who warns him that he has "one day to remedy the situation." The showgirls lead the way to Bushnell's office. "We come bearing gifts," Candie says (invoking the Three Wise Men), and presents Dougie's boss with monogrammed diamond cufflinks. Clad in identical pink gowns, gloves and jewelery, they resemble a Warholian triplicate of Marilyn Monroe when she sang 'Diamonds Are a Girl's Best Friend' in *Gentlemen Prefer Blondes*. In the *Twin Peaks* universe, the girls' strapless tutus also resemble Laura Palmer's bandeau prom dress.

At Dougie's family home on Lancelot court, delivery men bring a new car—wrapped in a red ribbon—and a 'gym set' (or swing set) for Sonny Jim. That night, he runs through its golden arch, the set now assembled and lit. "Sonny Jim's in seventh heaven," Janey-E tells Dougie (in contrast to the "ninth circle of hell" inhabited by Audrey Horne.)

At a warehouse in Western Montana, Ray Monroe watches Mr. C (Cooper's double, played by Kyle MacLachlan) approach via surveillance camera, and realizes that his former boss has survived his murder attempt. "You didn't kill him too good, Ray," jeers his new boss, the tall, bald Renzo (Derek Mears.) Mr. C explains that he wants to see Ray alone. By then, a crowd has gathered. "This man is our boss because no one can beat him at arm-wrestling. It's real simple," explains Renzo's right-hand man, Muddy (Frank Collison.) So if Mr. C wants Ray, he'll have to beat Renzo first. "What is this, kindergarten? Nursery school?" retorts Mr. C, unimpressed. "I don't want to be your boss," he adds, but takes the challenge. As Mr. C walks towards a table, Renzo punches the back of his head: "That was from the nursery school teacher." (Among the curious onlookers is Richard Horne, hiding out after his assault on a nursery school teacher.) Facing each other, the men take up 'starting positions', and as Renzo's gang cheer him on, it looks like Mr. C has been outclassed. But he quickly reveals unnatural strength, sadistically forcing his opponent back to 'starting positions'. "It hurt my arm when you moved it down there," Mr. C tells Renzo (echoing Laura's long-ago red room remark: "I feel like I know her, but sometimes my arms bend back.") Finally he punches Renzo in the face, which melts like Bill Hastings' as he falls to the ground. "He's all yours, boss," Muddy says, as Ray tries to make his escape. Mr. C orders the men to give him their phones, and throws them out. Only a bespectacled accountant (Christopher Durbin) lingers, and seemingly unafraid, asks, "Do you need any money?"

Alone with Ray, Mr C. says, "Somebody hired you to kill me." "It came through a man called Phillip Jeffries. I never met him," Ray admits. "You've got something inside that they want." He hands Mr. C a jade ring, given to him by a guard at Yankton Prison ("I never saw him before.") Telling Mr. C that Jeffries never mentioned Major Briggs, he says the long-lost FBI agent is probably at 'The Dutchman's' – "not the real place," he adds. Ray plays his trump card: "You want the co-ordinates I got from Hastings—or rather his pretty secretary, Betty?" (This may be an oblique reference to Betty Briggs, widow of Major Briggs whom Hastings had encountered before his demise.) As soon as he hands over the slip of paper, Mr. C shoots Ray, and places the ring on his finger. Ray is transported to the red room, entombed in a pool of blood.

At the Las Vegas Police Department, the three Fusco brothers (referencing J.C. Duffy's comic strip of the same name) arrange to meet for Sunday lunch at their mother's house ("Hope there's no murders this weekend.") As before, they ignore the commotion in an adjoining room, where a woman is pleading, "We want to report a cop." Detective D. Fusco (David Koechner) produces the results of DNA testing on a coffee mug used by Dougie Jones. After he reads out the report – identifying Dougie as an FBI agent, recently escaped from prison – the brothers erupt with mirth, and toss the evidence in a wastepaper basket.

Outside, Anthony Sinclair talks to Detective Clark (John Savage), who is taking a cigarette break. Like Mr. Todd, Clark treats Anthony with contempt. "Why are you so against me?" Anthony whines, repeating Chad Broxford's complaints to his colleagues in Twin Peaks. After he leaves, Clark tells a crony that he's going to call Mr. Todd. In Lynch's Las Vegas, police corruption clearly runs much deeper than the Fusco brothers' ineptitude.

Still on the road, Chantal and Hutch cross the Utah state line and crack Mormon jokes. In Twin Peaks, a worried Becky calls Shelly from her trailer, telling her that Steven has been missing for two days: "He's going through something bad, I can feel it." At work in the RR Diner, Shelly promises her daughter pie if she joins her there, and Becky can't resist. (Whether Becky ever made it is unclear, as she won't be seen again.)

Back in Las Vegas, Janey drives Dougie to work in their new car. A nervous Anthony meets him outside the offices of Lucky 7, and makes an offer Dougie can't refuse. They sit down for coffee outside Szymon's Café (the same chain used in New York by the ill-fated Tracey, when she bought coffees to share with Sam in the glass-box room.) Spying pie on the counter, Dougie wanders inside while Anthony slips a poisoned vial into his drink. After a kindly waitress (Virginia Kull) offers to bring the pie over, Dougie returns to Anthony. Noticing flecks of white powder on his jacket collar, Dougie picks at the fabric. This reduces Anthony to tears and he runs away, flushing the poisoned coffee in the bathroom sink.

"I've been selling you down the river," Anthony confesses to Mullins. "I've lied and cheated for money." (His voice is now at the same hysterical pitch as Hastings during his confession to Tammy.) "My anger, my contempt for you is subsiding," Bushnell replies fiercely. "If it weren't for Dougie, I might have a murder on my hands." As Dougie looks on, Anthony finally agrees to testify against Mr. Todd: "I only want to die, or change!" Although his future looks bleak—the two cops he spoke to earlier are "worse than Todd"—Anthony gets down on his knees and thanks Dougie for "saving my life."

When Bobby arrives at the RR Diner at night, his ex-wife and daughter are nowhere to be seen. After ordering "the usual," he notices Ed Hurley (Everett Gill) chatting with

Norma Jennings (Peggy Lipton) in a booth. "It's no good eating alone," Ed says in his distinctive baritone, and Bobby joins them. The bonhomie fizzles when sharp-suited Walter (Grant Goodeve) arrives to talk business. Ed and Bobby move to another booth, and as Ed fondly watches a smiling Norma, it seems their decades-long love affair is no closer to resolution. If Ed could hear their conversation, however, he would know Norma's smile isn't genuine.

Walter talks about their franchise they're building, telling her, "You're spending too much per pie, and not charging enough." At the RR, she says, all ingredients are organic and locally sourced; but although she has shared her recipe with other branches, they aren't following her instructions. Walter suggests "tweaking the formula" and renaming the RR 'Norma's Double R.' "In Twin Peaks, it's been the RR Diner for fifty years," she protests. "Norma," Walter sighs, "you're a real artist. But love doesn't always turn a profit." (Norma's predicament seems to mirror Lynch's precarious status as an avant-garde filmmaker in Hollywood.)

In the 'Run Silent, Run Drapes' shop window, a golden shovel glimmers, and then disappears as the curtains are drawn. A dungaree-clad Lawrence Jacoby is filling his truck with groceries when he notices his creation, and rings the buzzer. Nadine Hurley answers: "Dr. Amp!" she greets him, beaming. "Thanks to you," she says gaily, "I'm really starting to shovel myself out of the shit." "It's us against them," he stammers, and Nadine declares herself "your loyal foot-soldier." Many years ago, when Nadine suffered her first breakdown, she was assessed by Dr. Jacoby (his report is published in *The Secret History of Twin Peaks*.) Jacoby remembers the last time he saw her, "down on your knees in the supermarket, looking for a potato"—and they glance at each other coyly. (Will these two eccentrics find happiness at last? In *Twin Peaks: The Final Dossier*, Mark Frost suggests they just might.)

At the Palmer house, a lonely Sarah watches the same clip from an old boxing match on a loop, occasionally leaving the room to replenish her Bloody Marys. In *The Final Dossier*, Frost tells us that she grew up in New Mexico, where her father was a government employee on the Manhattan Project. In the pivotal eighth episode of the series, Lynch depicts the historic nuclear tests in the desert, and as woodsmen terrorize nearby residents, a sinister 'frog-moth' climbs into the mouth of a young girl, dreaming of her kiss. Was the boy who walked her home that evening a young 'Battling Bud' Mullins, and is Sarah now thinking of what could have been?

Across the forest, Audrey and Charlie have put on their coats and are standing by their front door, but something prevents them from leaving. This suggests a 'dweller on the threshold', which Hawk once mentioned was part of Nez Perce mythology. The dweller represents the negative forces within a person, which must be confronted as they approach enlightenment. "I feel like I'm somewhere else and someone else," Audrey tells Charlie, who glibly summarizes her plight as "Existentialism 101." "I don't know who I am, but I'm not me," she goes on, but Charlie can't relate: "I always feel like myself, and it's not always the best feeling." Wearily, he hangs up his coat, and Audrey follows him into a living room. "Are you going to stop playing games," he warns, "or do I have to end your story?" Audrey taunts him: "What story is that, Charlie? Is it the story of the little girl who lives down the lane?" She finally breaks down, sobbing, "It's like Ghostwood in here." (At the end of Season 2, a young Audrey was critically injured in a bank explosion after chaining herself to a vault, in protest at her father Ben Horne's plans to redevelop the forest.)

We return to the Roadhouse, where James Hurley (James Marshall) sings 'You and I', backed by two girl singers. He first performed Lynch's ballad in the original series, with his babyish vocals echoed by Donna Hayward and Maddy Ferguson. We first glimpsed the older James when he waved to Shelly and her friends in the red booth. The other women laughed, calling him crazy (in *The Final Dossier*, Frost reveals that before his return to Twin Peaks James had fallen off his motorcycle, suffering a severe head injury.) Shelly smiles broadly at him, saying, "James is cool. James has always been cool." And though James has been derided by some fans, it seems Lynch feels the same. As he sings, a pretty woman named Renee (Jessica Szhor) weeps copiously, and then turns to an unseen companion with a forced smile.

In this episode's closing frames, James' equally luckless uncle sits alone in Big Ed's Gas Farm, miserably supping on takeout soup from the RR and watching cars drive by. After a few moments, the passing traffic seems to loop, another sign that time is in flux. As Ed gazes listlessly ahead, we notice a rather ugly toy bear on his desk (not unlike the therapeutic toy given to Johnny Horne.) Next to it, a sign spells out Lynch's message to us: "BEAR WITH ME."

Jackrabbit's Palace
The voice of Gordon Cole blasts down the line to the Sheriff's Station in Twin Peaks. "Lucy?" he marvels, "you've been there all through the years?" She connects him to Frank Truman and after passing on good wishes to Harry, Cole hears about the recovered missing pages of Laura Palmer's diary, and the possibility of two Coopers. Although he can't explain why it is useful, he thanks Frank for the information. We then return to his hotel suite in Buckhorn, now converted into a makeshift office complete with blue screens and transmitters which he tunes into regularly.

In a motel in Olympia, Washington in 1975, Gordon and Philip Jeffries found a dying woman who smiled and said, "I am like the blue rose", and vanished before their eyes. An identical woman, Lois Duffy, was also in the room. While awaiting trial for murder, she hung herself. Albert relates this to Tammy: "A blue rose does not occur in nature," she observes. "The dying woman was conjured – a *tulpa*." (As explained in *The Final Dossier*, the 'tulpa' is a concept borrowed from Eastern mysticism and later adopted by American theosophists in the late nineteenth century.)

Cole is disturbed by the scrapings of a window cleaner from outside, which we hear at the same high volume as the partially deaf FBI agent. 'Deputy Diane' arrives, "reporting for duty" with a mock salute. She still refuses to discuss the last time she saw Cooper (before his disappearance) but admits to Cole that he mentioned Major Briggs that night. Briggs died in a fire at a government facility twenty-five years ago, Gordon relates to the group, but his headless body was found only recently, with a ring inside his stomach inscribed, "To Dougie, from Janey-E."

Janey Evans is her half-sister, Diane tells the group, and she lives in Las Vegas with her husband, Dougie Jones. "We're estranged," Diane says, adding, "I hate her."

"Last night I had another Monica Bellucci dream," Cole continues, and Albert groans. The Italian star of *The Matrix* appears as herself, as we enter Gordon's dream in black-and-white. They were sitting outside a café in Paris, he tells us, and Cooper was nearby though his face remains unseen. "And then," Cole explains, "She said the ancient phrase: *'We are like the dreamer who dreams, then lives inside the dream ... But who is the dreamer?'"* (This quotation has its roots within the Upanishads, the Sanskrit writings which have influenced Buddhism and other religions.)

Monica indicated that he should look back. "A very powerful, uneasy feeling came over me," Cole recalls. "I saw myself a long time ago..." A crucial scene from *Fire Walk With Me* is replayed, with a younger Cole at FBI HQ in Philadelphia. Cooper is telling him about a dream he had when a disorientated Phillip Jeffries (David Bowie) enters the room, points at Cooper and says *"Now who do you think that is there?"* before vanishing again. "Damn, I hadn't remembered that," Cole says as the dream recedes; and Albert, who was also in the room, adds: "I'm beginning to remember that too."

Over at the Sheriff's Station, the team are preparing to visit 'Jackrabbit's Palace', the location where Major Briggs took his son Bobby as a child. Chad Broxford bursts into the conference room, and Hawk points his gun. Frank arrests Chad, and as Deputy Andy Brennan (Harry Goaz) takes him down to the holding cell, Chad rages: "You're making a big mistake." Andy rejoins the others and they drive to Ghostwood Forest. "We'd sit here and make up great, tall tales," Bobby reminisces, "but my father told me never to wander around here without him."

As they reach Jackrabbit's Palace, the men notice a cloud of smoke around a circle of trees. Naido (Nae Yuuki), the eyeless woman who led Cooper out of the glass box building, lies there naked, but alive. Andy feels the pulse of her hand, and looks up at the tornado above them. He vanishes, and reappears in what looks like the old movie palace from Part 8. The spirit formerly known as the Giant raises his hand, and says: "I am the Fireman." Andy looks up into a rounded porthole, and sees a series of images. First up is the Experiment, a ghostly figure which in the season's opener, emerged from a glass box to murder two young lovers. This is followed by several familiar motifs from the original series, such as the rustling red curtains, and a girl running across the high-school lawn. Andy sees Laura, surrounded by angels; the two Coopers; and himself, comforting wife Lucy.

Back in the forest, Andy carries Naido and tells the others: "We need to get her down the mountain; she's very important and there are people who want her dead. Don't tell anybody about this." At the Sheriff's Station, he takes her to a cell where Lucy gently dresses her in pink pyjamas. (This choice of clothing evokes an old folk song, 'She'll Be Coming Round the Mountain," in which "She'll be wearing pink pyjamas when she comes." 'She' refers to the heavenly chariot which brings the end of the world, or rapture.)

"You're no kind of cop at all," Chad sneers from Cell 10 as Andy leaves. "You give good policemen a bad name!" he replies. Their words are parroted by a drunk with a mutilated face in Cell 5 (Jay Aaseng), who also mimics Naido's bird-like twittering. "Shut up, you fucking drunk!" Chad yells. This may be the same drunk Chad picked up on the road a few nights ago, or even the same drunk who ran Trick into a ditch. It's James Hurley's birthday, and he's sitting outside the Great Northern Hotel with fellow security guard Freddie Sykes, a young Cockney played by Jake Wardle (a YouTube star with a gift for accents.) Although Wardle hails from East London, Freddie's accent is as exaggerated as Dick Van Dyke's in *Mary Poppins*. (His name was probably inspired by the late British actor Freddie Jones, who became one of Lynch's regular players after appearing in *The Elephant Man*, the Oscar-nominated biopic set in a Dickensian East End.) Freddie's voice isn't the strangest thing about him, however; that would be the green gardening glove attached to his right hand. "It's part of me," he says, but James wants to know more: "It's my birthday, you've got to tell me."

While walking home from the pub one night, Freddie had an epiphany. "I'm wastin' me life," he thought. "I should be 'elping people." He climbed on top of a stack of boxes in an alley, and was swept into a vortex by a giant who called himself 'The Fireman', and told him to buy a single green glove from a torn packet in the local hardware store. Pausing for levity, Freddie riffs on The Beatles' 'Day in the Life', saying, "Woke up, got out of bed/Dragged a comb across my head…"

The cashier in the hardware store—a "jobsworth," in Freddie's words—refused to sell him the glove; so he grabbed it, left the money by the till, and "ran like a possessed puma." After he put on the glove, the "bloke in the sky" reappeared, telling him to go to Twin Peaks and "find your destiny." When Freddie asked, "Why me?", the Fireman replied, "Why not?" Perhaps Deputy Andy was chosen for the same reason. Dumbstruck, James goes into the hotel's boiler room to check the furnace. The faint ringing sound heard by Ben and Beverly upstairs is even louder there.

The Green Man is a central figure in English folklore, while 'green fingers' is a phrase used to describe someone with a gift for gardening. In his 2017 memoir, *Room to Dream*, Lynch reveals that the 'green glove' concept was designed for the late character actor Jack Nance, who starred in Lynch's debut feature, *Eraserhead* (1977) and in *Twin Peaks* as Pete Martell, who died in the bank explosion during the second season's finale. The Elk's Point #9 Bar has the same red neon logo as the Roadhouse, and Max Von's Bar in Philadelphia, where Albert found Diane. With shapeless attire, the figure seen walking into Elk's Point could be a woodsman. In fact, it's Sarah Palmer. She bypasses the pool table and orders a Bloody Mary while a trucker (John Paulsen) leers at her. He wears a baseball cap, and his T-shirt reads 'TRUCK YOU'. We're reminded of what Mr. C's associate, Buella, once said: "It's a world of truck drivers." Sarah asks the trucker to leave her alone, but he continues harassing her: "It's a free *cunt*-ry."

With a low growl, this frail-looking woman asks, "Do you really want to fuck with this?" Her face is an open door, like Laura's in the red room; but there is no light in Sarah's face, and a grey X-Ray negative of her daughter's mouth grins back hideously at the truck driver. It seems that darkness has finally claimed Sarah's spirit; as the trucker stares back, she rips his head off. Her face returns to normal, and she lets out a scream. The bartender looks down at the man's dead body, and glances at Sarah, who says with a smirk: "Sure is a mystery, huh?"

In the red booth at the Roadhouse, two young women are talking. Megan (Shane Lynch) is telling Sophie (played by Lynch's wife, Emily Stofle) about the last time she saw Billy. Sophie's questions are leading, and she seems more like a detective than a concerned friend. "He was bleeding from the nose and mouth," Megan says, echoing Audrey's dream. "He ran out again—I don't remember if my uncle was there …" Billy and her mom "had a thing," Megan admits, and Sophie asks her mother's name. It's Tina, the same woman Audrey loathes and who swore Charlie to secrecy.

If these Roadhouse scenes have little apparent connection to the Twin Peaks we know, they are now bringing us closer to Audrey's inner life. The episode plays out with Lissie's raw rendition of 'Wild West', voicing the pain and anger of women like Sarah and Audrey, and the loneliness and heartache of men like Ed and Bobby which continues to haunt Twin Peaks.

TARA HANKS WAS BORN AND RAISED IN LONDON. SINCE THEN SHE HAS LIVED IN LANCASTER, DERBY AND NOW BRIGHTON. SHE IS MARRIED AND HAS TWO SONS.

WICKED BABY, TARA'S NOVELLA BASED ON THE EVENTS OF THE PROFUMO AFFAIR, WAS PUBLISHED IN 2004. AN EXTRACT HAS BEEN SHOWCASED ON THE OFFICIAL WEBSITE OF WHITBREAD-NOMINATED AUTHOR LAURA HIRD.

THE MMM GIRL, TARA'S NOVEL ABOUT THE LIFE OF MARILYN MONROE, WINNER OF THE UKA PRESS OPENING PAGES COMPETITION, AND WAS PUBLISHED IN 2007. EXTRACTS FROM IT ARE FEATURED IN VOICES FROM THE WEB ANTHOLOGY 2006 AND FAN PHENOMENA: MARILYN MONROE.

CO-AUTHORED WITH ERIC WOODARD, JEANNE EAGELS, FIRST FULL-SCALE BIOGRAPHY OF THE LEGENDARY ACTRESS IN MORE THAN EIGHTY YEARS, WAS PUBLISHED IN 2015.

TARA ALSO WRITES ABOUT ASPECTS OF POPULAR CULTURE FOR A VARIETY OF WEBSITES AND PUBLICATIONS (INCLUDING FOR BOOKS' SAKE, IMMORTAL MARILYN AND ART DECADES) AND MAINTAINS THE ES UPDATES BLOG. SHE IS CURRENTLY WORKING ON HER THIRD NOVEL.

FROM TARAHANKS.COM

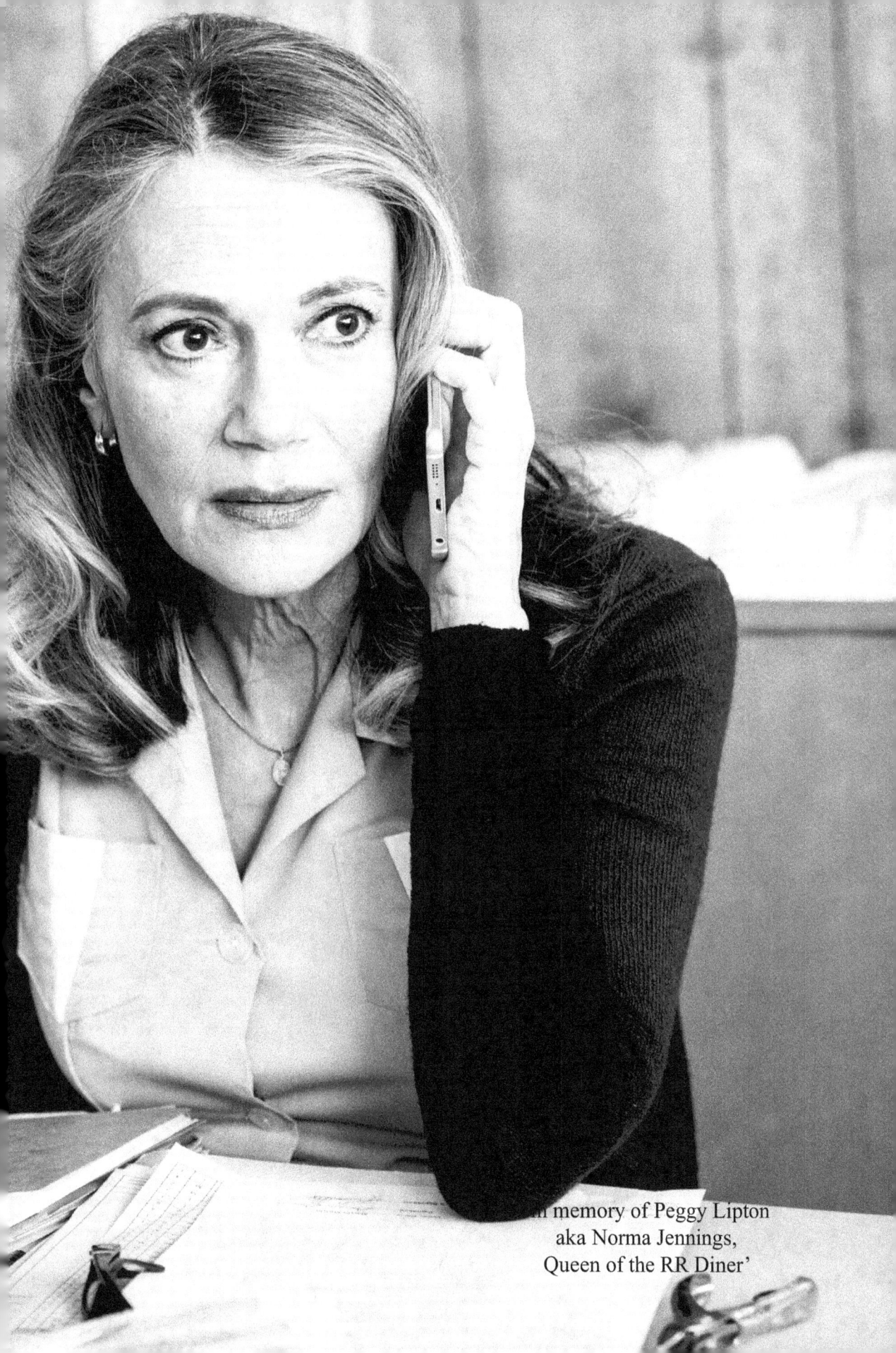

In memory of Peggy Lipton
aka Norma Jennings,
Queen of the RR Diner'

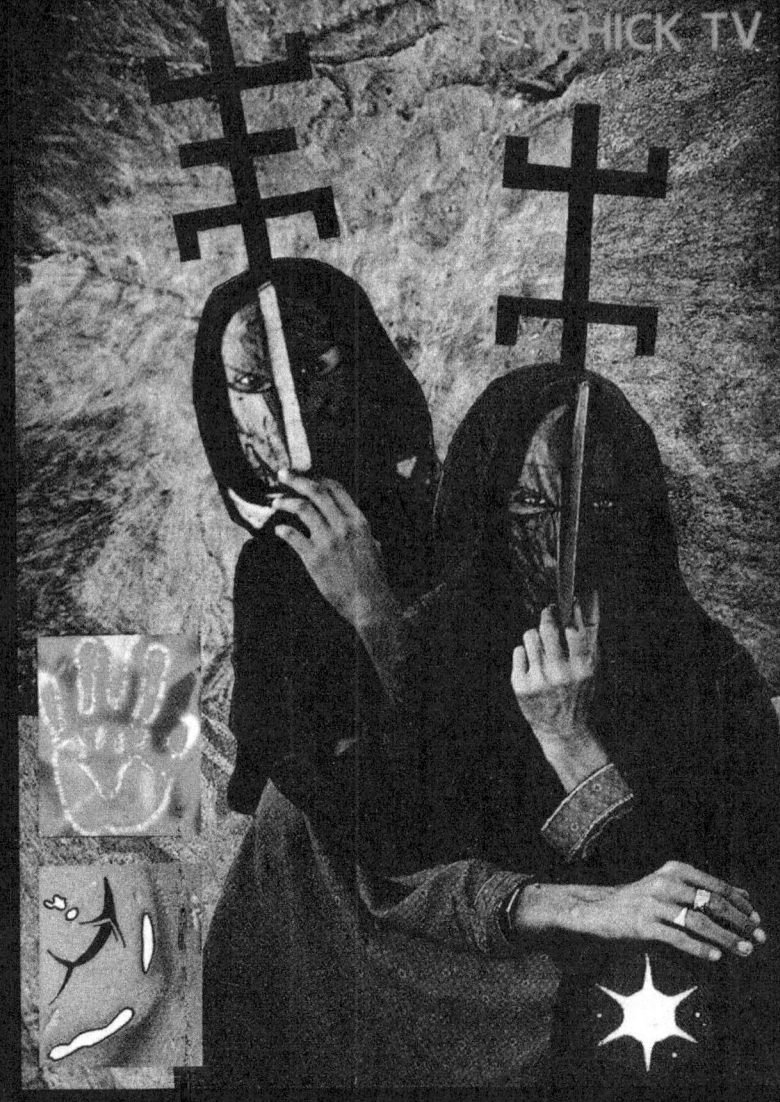

KONDOLE

PSYCHICK TV

Available on Cassette,
LP and Compact Disc
from
Temple Records

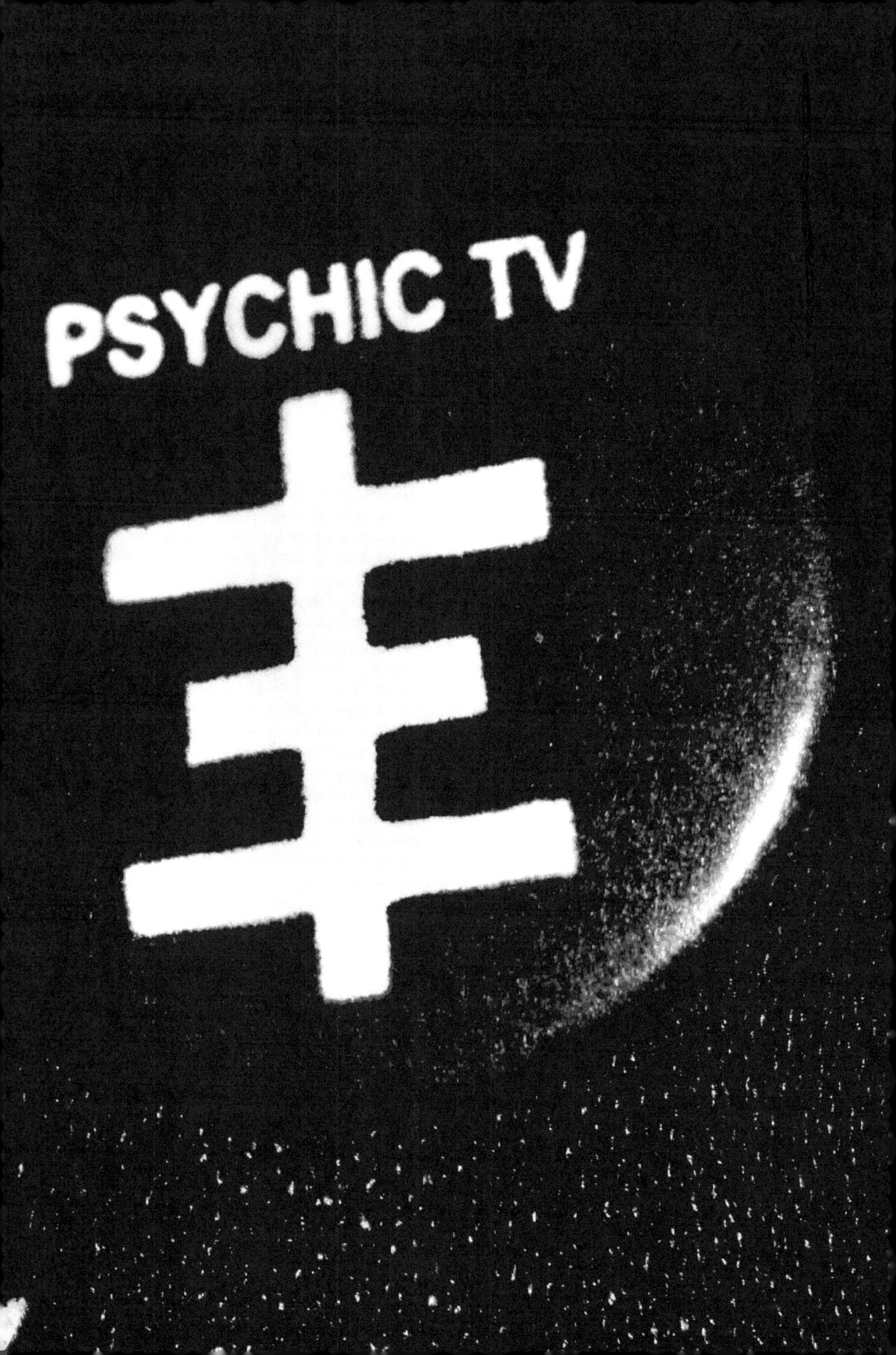
PSYCHIC TV

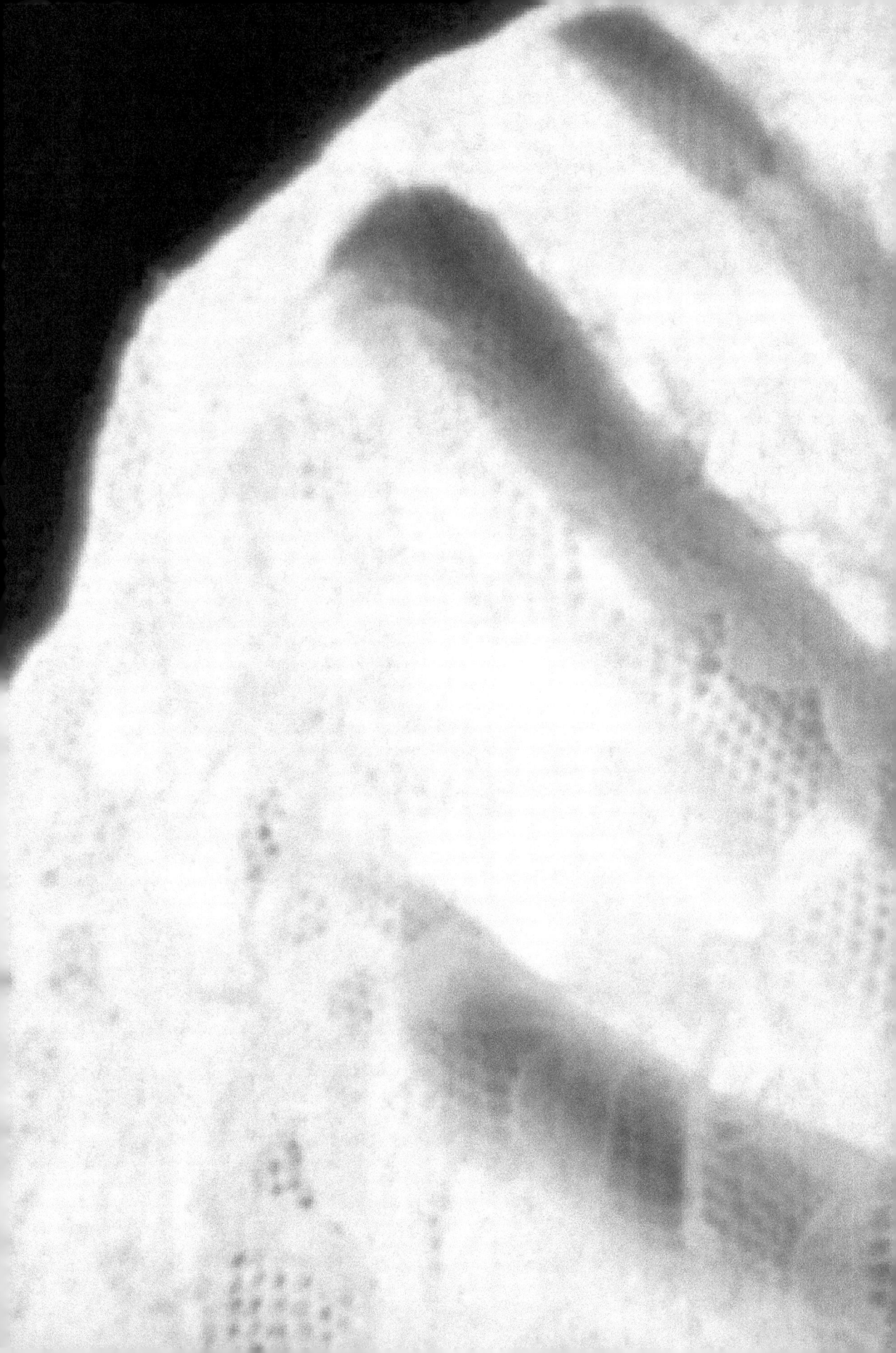

EMERGING ARTISTS

By

John David Levy

IN 2013 I CONDUCTED AN INTERVIEW FOR
ART DECADES, ANOTHER NOSTALGIA KINKY PUBLICATION, WITH
INDEPENDENT FILM PRODUCER KIM SHERMAN.
THE PIECE FOCUSED ON HER
JOURNEY PRODUCING SOME OF THE BEST FILMS TO EMERGE FROM THE
LATE OUGHTS INTO THE TWO THOUSAND TEENS,
(SUN DON'T SHINE, YOU'RE NEXT, A TEACHER, ONE & TWO),
AND THE RISE OF SO MANY WOMEN
ON THE CREATIVE FRONT OF INDIE FILM.

SINCE THEN WE'VE SEEN TREMENDOUS CHANGE AND THE WOMEN WHO
CAME OUT OF THE DIY NO BUDGET GENERATION HAVE ALL GONE ON TO
PAVE A NEW FRONTIER FOR WOMEN IN FILM AND
CONTINUE TO PRODUCE SOME OF THE MOST
EVOCATIVE AND POLARIZING CINEMATIC ART TODAY.
ALONG WITH SHERMAN WE SAW INDIE ARTISTS LIKE AMY SIEMETZ, BRIT
MARLING, MEGAN GRIFFITHS, LYNNE SHELTON, KELLY RICHARDT, JOSEPHINE
DECKER, HANNAH FIDELL, DEBRA GRANICK, MIRANDA JULY
AND NUMEROUS OTHERS
CONTINUE TO CHANGE THE FACE OF WHERE FILM CAN GO,
WHAT WE HAVEN'T EXPLORED AND HOW WE CAN EXPLORE IT.

AS WE CLOSE THIS CRAZY DECADE AND HEAD TOWARD THE NEXT AND
ARGUABLY THE MOST IMPORTANT ON EVERY FRONT, I SEE A NEW
EMERGENCE OF RESONATING ARTISTRY IN THE CINEMATIC LANDSCAPE,
PARTICULARLY FROM WOMEN AND ESPECIALLY FROM
NON-COMMERCIAL, STUDENT FILMMAKERS AND AN ALMOST NEW
AMERICAN AVANT-GARDE WHERE MULTIPLE DISCIPLINES ARE APPLIED AND
VERY SINGULAR VOICES ARE FOUND.

IN THIS PIECE I WANT TO HIGHLIGHT TWO OF MY FAVORITE FILMMAKERS
WORKING IN SHORT FORM, OUTSIDE OF STANDARD NARRATIVE,
DOCUMENTARY OR EVEN EXPERIMENTAL FILM
AS WE'VE KNOWN THIS DECADE. BOTH THESE
ARTISTS WORKS EXIST ON A BLURRED LINE OF GENRE AND FORMAT. BOTH
ARE YOUNG AND HAVE ONLY BEEN PRODUCING FILMS IN
RECENT YEARS AND HAVE GENERATED SOME OF THE MOST INDELIBLE,
EXPERIMENTAL NO- TO- LOW BUDGET EARLY WORKS I'VE SEEN IN SOME
TIME. I'M PARTICULARLY GEARED TOWARDS ART AND ARTISTS WHOSE
WORK I WALK AWAY FROM WITH SOMETHING I DIDN'T WALK INTO IT WITH.
WHOSE VISIONS, WORDS, MOVEMENTS, AMBIANCE STAYS WITH ME AND IS
NOT EASILY LABELED.

THESE QUALITIES I FIND IN THE CREATIONS OF
SOPHIA GRIMANI AND GILLIAN WALDO.

SOPHIA GRIMANI

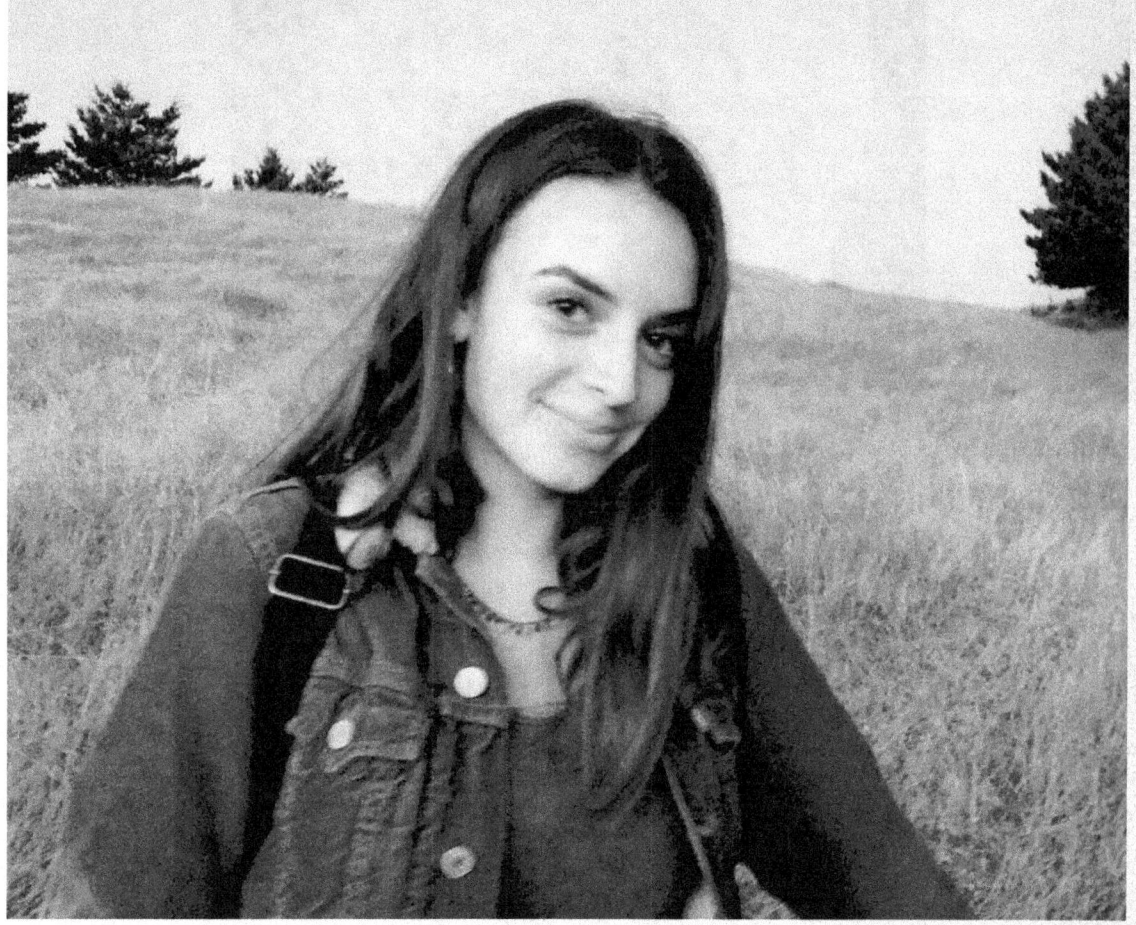

Filmmaker, choreographer, dancer and photographer Sophia Grimani has unfolded an incredible cinematic journey in just a few years. With a decade and a half of discipline in the art of dance and a photographic portfolio that evokes the scent of emulsion mixed with the nostalgia of ocean air, bond fires on the beach, aquatic excursions and sunsets on the mountain top, cinema has become a wide open frontier for Grimani's visions and movements to come together. I've had the privilege of working with Grimani and when kicking ideas around with her and discussing cinema it was very apparent I was talking to a natural born artist. Meaning; She didn't just fall into it, it's her life blood. She's serious and passionate about it, but she is also finding necessary pleasure in creation. It's a conduit of her being. And that is clear in her work. When I was introduced to her very first forays into filmmaking it was not what I expected. When I think of my or most filmmakers very first works, I shutter with endearment, but out the gate, her films were on fire, and the progression from the first to second was revelatory, because of how few filmmakers are that pronounced and singular from the start as well as how few filmmakers or artists we witness at such a place in their evolution. This makes her a very exciting creator to watch. Each discipline informs the other in the way nature's elements work together. Her use of audio testimonials and central themes transcend any one format. This is beautifully portrayed in some of her earlier works. One in particular, features a group of dancers in white, first dancing around some graffitied abandoned facilities being reclaimed by nature and then moving further out to grand landscapes of environments in full bloom. All playing out to Debussy's 'Claire de Lune' and interspersed with voiceover from the dancers meditating on their passion and thirst for dance. The brush strokes of this visual piece translate to her choreography as well.

In a stunning piece she choreographed entitled *Love*, she again applies voiceover, this time in live performance, exploring the central theme through intimate testimonial that evokes color, memory and butterflies in the belly. This harmony of arts presents a narrative in the body of work just as there is a narrative of body in dance. It's all specific to her while being wholly and completely universal.

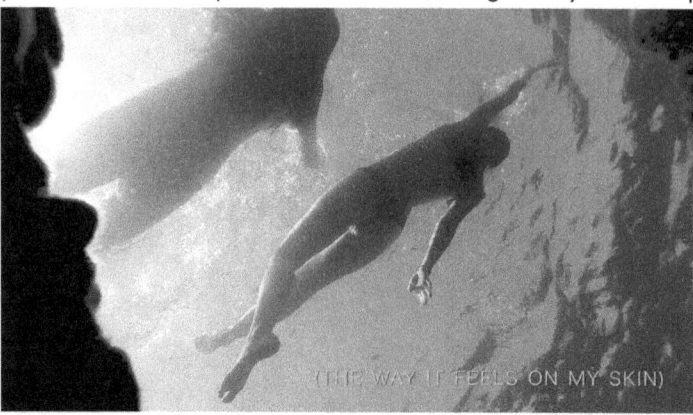

(THE WAY IT FEELS ON MY SKIN)

We are witnessing the evolution of a woman through the evolution of her art. Thus far, this is best exhibited in her most recent work, *A Sense of Sensuality*. What the title promises the film gushes in a sensory mosaic. A meditation on touch, texture and movement featuring testimonials on intimacy, dopaminal symbolism and a sound design that puts you inside its subject, thematics and creator.
Culminating in a crystallized exhibit of the elements found in her previous work,
A Sense of Sensuality marks a crucial moment in Grimani's artistic evolution of what came before and what will come next. Grimani cultivates the content of her films, and really all of her work, with a nurturing patience. Coming away from my first viewing of *A Sense of Sensuality* and discussing it with a fellow filmmaker, my reaction reminded them of the lore behind the Mayoruna hallucinatory Sapo ritual from which one is said to emerge with their senses completely reset. In an age of technological entropy and disconnection, I came away from *A Sense of Sensuality* with not so much a physical reset of the senses as a reset of awareness of them and a feeling of connection to all things. It gave me a desire for intimacy and flavor as well as solitary exploration, introspection and meditation on my own creations and an impulse to look deeper at the details and allow the whimsy of what's beyond my free will to rush over me.
Discovery, or more over, rediscovery.

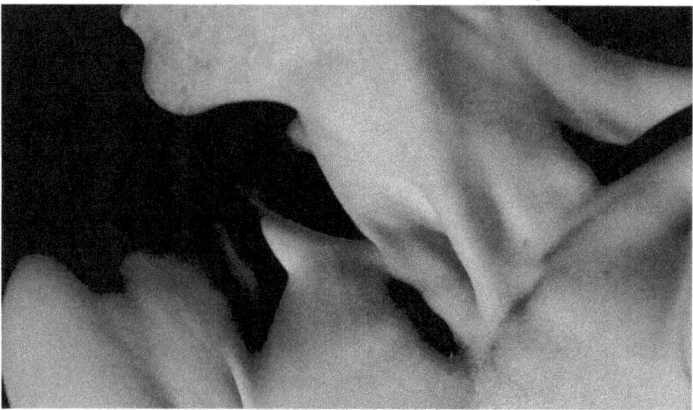

Grimani's creative contributions to my film *The Disappearance,* and collaboration on *Eons of Sunsets Have Nothing on You*, opened my eyes to what dance could bring to film from behind the camera and in the stories that bleed from the pen. My time working with her was the most enriching and creatively satisfying filmmaking experience because I was collaborating with an artist I not only respect but who also inspires and the biggest takeaway from that was to always strive to work with creators of that caliber. Hopefully I will have the good fortune to collaborate with Grimani again. The future of art films holds one certainty; We should all look forward to what Sophia Grimani produces in the decade to come.
A Sense of Sensuality is streaming on Youtube and on Vimeo at : vimeo.com/306106084

GILLIAN WALDO

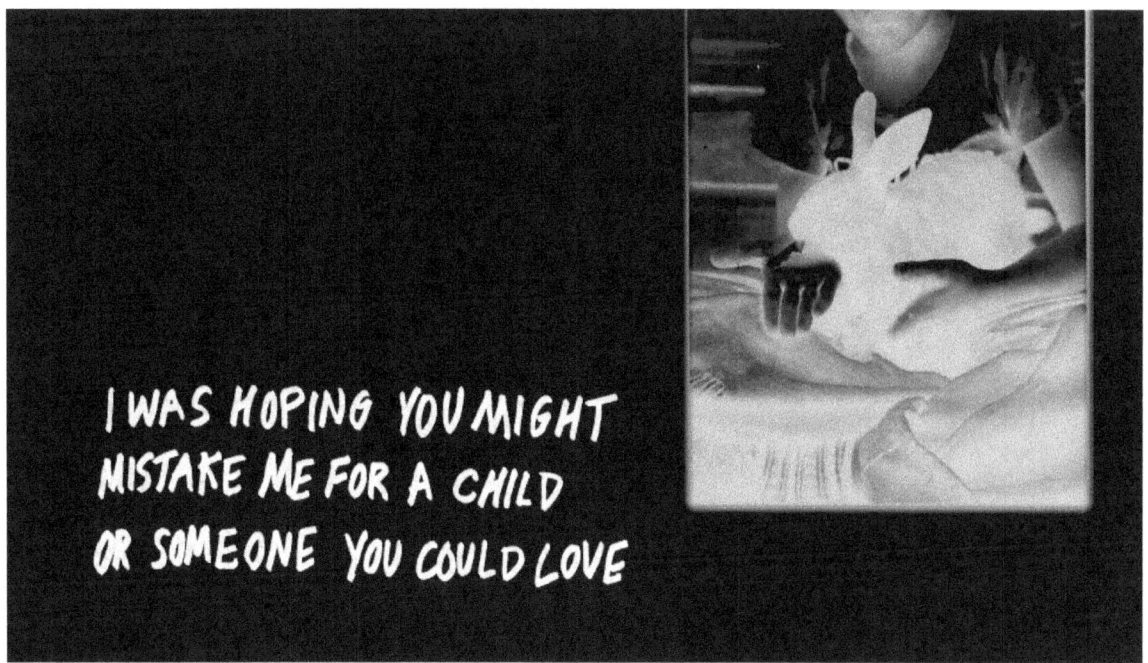

I WAS HOPING YOU MIGHT MISTAKE ME FOR A CHILD OR SOMEONE YOU COULD LOVE

Filmmaker Gillian Waldo, in just the last couple of years has put out an impressive body of work in the short form of film. Again, I don't wish to label this artist, but for the readers reference I suppose you'd see her films as experimental. Which they are. Waldo employs some of my favorite tools in her cinema. 16mm, hand written text, correspondence, photography, documentation, whispering, a kind of bold shyness, which is in itself kind of rare. She also works with really surprising and evoking sound designs. Her sound designs are the score to the films. These are all paintbrushes I enjoy using and experiencing in filmmaking, but Waldo is on another level. In her film *Go Tell Yer Brothers*, she uses Red handwritten text over a rapidly changing series of background slides of maps and photos to send a message to White Male America, "Dear White gentlemen of America / I see you in your Red caps." Sound design is especially impactful here set to a barrage of fireworks and gunshots, often indistinguishable, which may intentionally or unintentionally shed light on the American tradition of celebrating violence.

Her film *Leave No Trace* on the other hand, is carried by a whispering narrator and virtually no sound design save for a room or space tone that very much embodies the atmosphere, over 16mm Black and White footage reminiscent of what might have been if Francesca Woodman ever ventured deeper into filmmaking with her veiled images. The words of the piece are haunting and hit home. "Wherever I am, I am what's missing."

With *The Year My Teeth Fell Out* she once again employs the simple, yet thoughtful sound design of sneakers on the surface of the gym floor in what unfolds like an intimate letter or private entry written out on screen over Black and White X-Rays and inverted images, again, with haunting heart striking lines like, "I was standing in the corner watching you glow."

As a fellow artist and as her audience - I feel the same way.

Her most recent film *I Know What I Saw* is a travelogue of the American landscape, vanishing ways and worlds carried through intimate post card correspondence. Shot on 16mm and using stills and set to the sound of the barren midwest haunt of rodeos and neglected National Parks, Waldo brings a very powerful voice to certain issues without any pronounced political agenda.

When it's there it comes from an emotional and personal place. An observation on the American lie that shoulders racism and disappearing America.
There is a common thread of tone and style in her work yet no real trajectory to be seen, which makes the anticipation of what she'll create next all the more exciting.

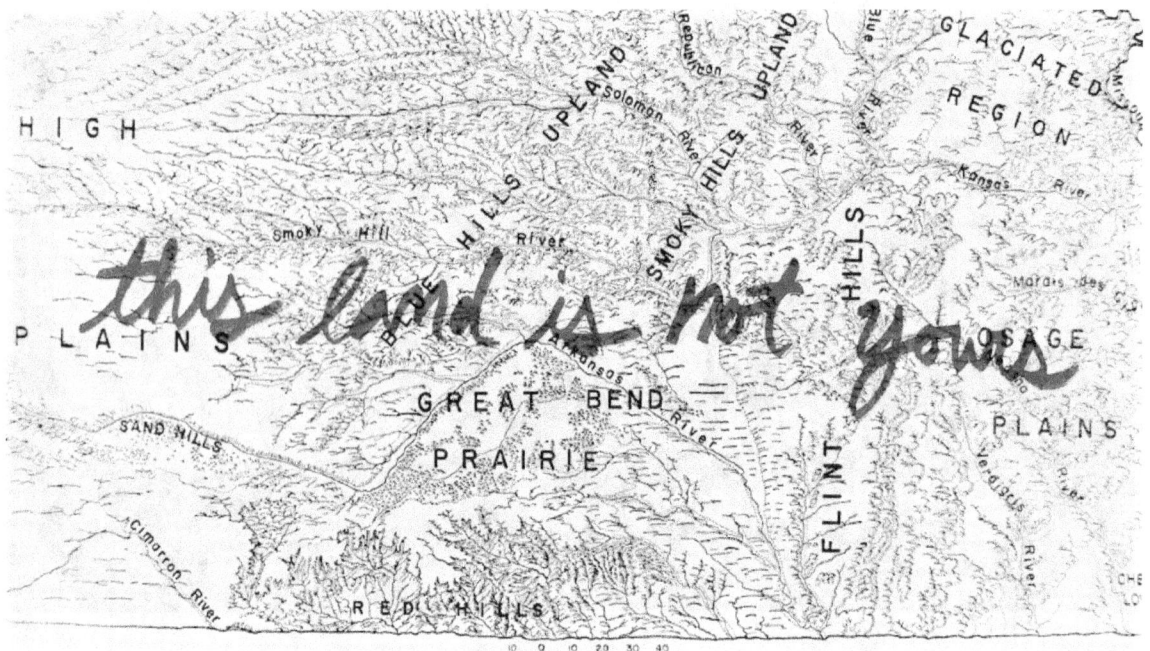

You can find Waldo's work on Vimeo at vimeo.com/gillianwaldo and her latest film
I Know What I Saw is currently featured on NoBudge.com

I CONSIDER MYSELF A MOTION PICTURE MAKER. BUT STILL PHOTOGRAPHY HAS BEEN PART OF MY LIFE AS LONG AS MOTION. AND MORE OFTEN THAN NOT THEY BLEED INTO EACH OTHER. I PICKED UP STILL PHOTOGRAPHY IN MY MID TEENS AROUND THE SAME TIME I BEGAN TO EXPERIMENT WITH FILM AND VIDEO. INSPIRED ACROSS BOTH FORMATS BY WORKS FROM RALPH STEINER TO FRANCESCA WOODMAN AND GORDON PARKS. AS A KID I'D LEAVE MY LOCAL MOVIE HOUSE AND TAKE A PHOTO WALK HOME. WHEN ON SET I TAKE AS MANY STILL AS POSSIBLE WHETHER WITH MY PHONE, CANONET OR DSLR. WHETHER IT'S MEDIUM FORMAT, 35MM, VIDEO OR SCREEN CAPTURES FROM MY VIDEOS, FROZEN OR
FLEETING - I'M ALWAYS MAKING PICTURES. AND I AM GRATEFUL TO HAVE A PLACE AND PEOPLE TO SHARE THEM WITH.

- JOHN DAVID LEVY

The Disappearance

a short film from JOHN LEVY

There are places on [...]
where time [...]
and space [...]
and ro[...]

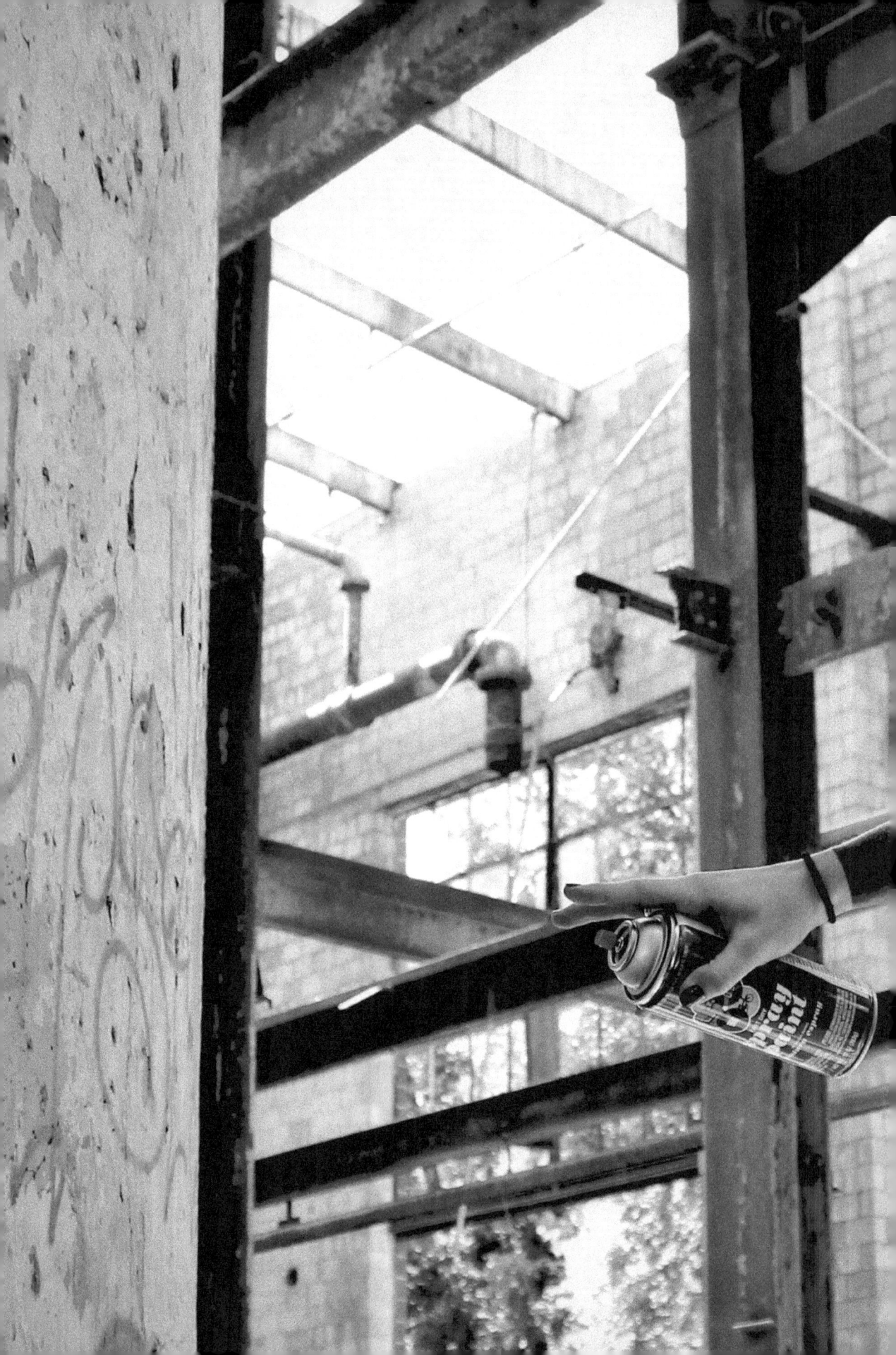

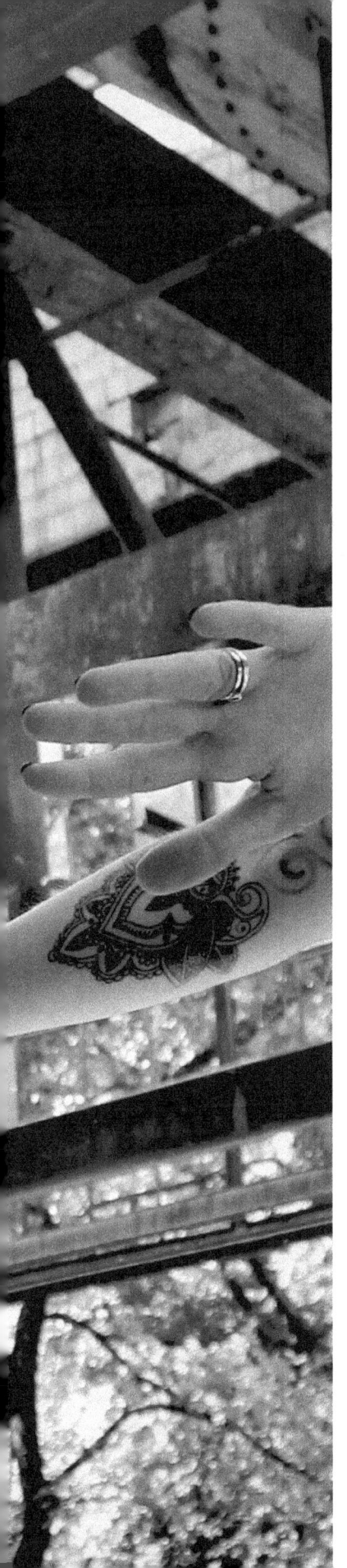

Graffiti City

by

Michael A. Gonzales

When I was a thirteen year old kid back in the summer of 1976, I truly believed my mom could see through walls. "Dorian Parker, if you fall out of that damn window I'm going to kill you!" she yelled over the smooth black velveteen vocals of Sammy Davis Jr.'s cloudy-sky crooning of "The Party's Over." For a moment I froze, wondering how mom always knew when I was doing stuff I wasn't supposed to be doing, especially looking out of living-room window.

In the make-believe ballroom of the living room, our old hi-fi constantly blasted the intoxicated Rat Pack boys whining into their vodka martinis. With the oversized television set in the corner, framed prints of bug-eyed Keane kids hanging on the beige wall, an olive-green sofa shrouded in sticky plastic and a wooden coffee table covered with back issues of *Ebony* and *Jet*, the living-room was always neat.

Leaning back from the soot smeared second floor window, my broken right arm hung close to my chest. The chalky cast that covered it was illustrated with the colorful graffiti tags of the neighborhood wild boys Voodoo Ray, C.C. and Smokey, the dudes who were my best friends. C.C., my best best friend, was the king of bombing, the best graffiti writer in the crew and everything we knew when it came to the craft he'd taught us. He'd tagged my cast in an ink so red and bright it reminded me of blood.

A hulking garbage truck crept down the steep hill. Dressed in dirty sanitation overalls, two dusty garbage men hung from the vomit-inducing stench of the dirty truck as the veteran driver mopped sweat from his brown brow. Leaping from the iron beast, the sweaty men swept the cluttered gutters polluted with broken beer, Wacky Packy wrappers and discarded nickel bag reefer sacks. With their fatheaded brooms, they swiftly swept both sides of the street as the sweet soul of Al Green drifted from a tattered portable radio tightly tied to one of the truck's back handles: "Simply beautiful," the lover man sang.

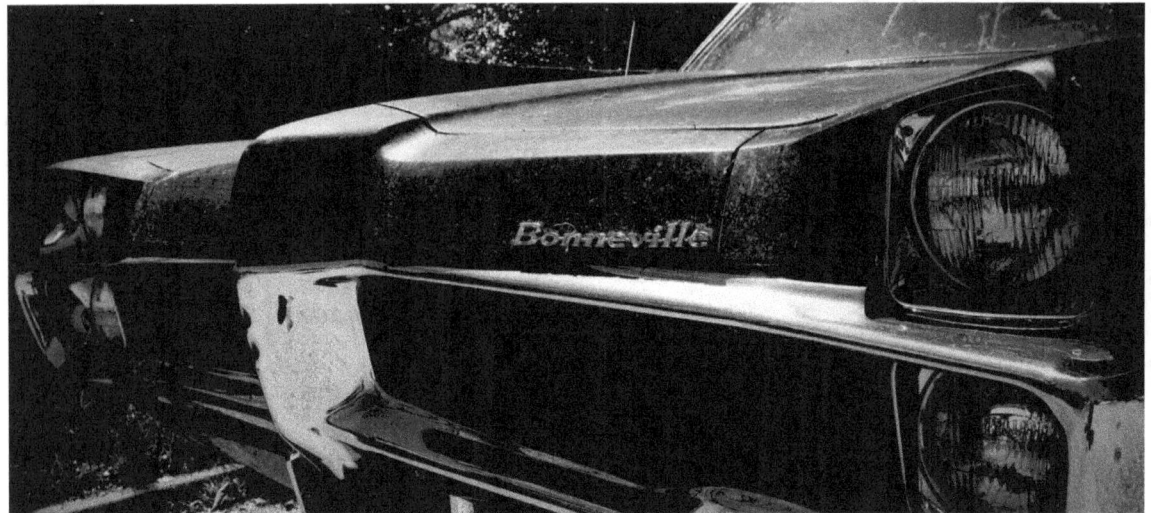

By eight o'clock every morning, 151st Street between Broadway and Riverside was already murmuring with an array of accents. Unlike some of them other sinful streets in Harlem, especially those overflowing with disreputable derelict corner-boys and simple-minded dope fiends who populated nasty S.R.O. flophouses, our block was considered pleasant. The folks that lived there were more like an extended family than a bunch of shady strangers. Indeed, our hood was crowded with first generation southern folks who had "come up north" thirty years past, a few old-school Jewish families who refused to move to the suburbs and a slow drizzle of Puerto Ricans and Dominicans.

As though struck by lightning, I suddenly remembered that it was the third Saturday in July and, as it been since I could remember, it was the day of our official city sanctioned Block Party. Nothing in the universe, with the exception of my grandma's death the year before, could have been as rough as me having to miss the wild uptown Mardi Gras of Block Party Day that would soon be happening outside. Beyond the police blue barricades halting traffic on the corner, bare-chested black boys splashed in the spraying fire hydrant while the girls marveled each other with double-dutch jump-rope tricks.

Later, one of the moms on the block would set-up a long cafeteria table stacked sky-high with tins of crispy fried chicken, buttery home-made cakes covered in colorful icings, Tupperware bowls overflowing with chunky potato salad and large tubs of sweet grape Kool-Aid mixed with ginger ale, all the kids would have worked-up a serious hunger.

"Come on, Ma, can't I just go outside for a little while?" I begged as crocodile tears rolled down my smooth cocoa face. Running away from the window, I flopped down in an over-stuffed chair pouting like a bad baby. So what if thirteen was too old to be begging, crying and whining like a baby, I was tired of staring at the black and white paisley wallpaper, and the tacky rainbow colored ashtrays on one of the end tables.

After days of being holed-up in the crib, even my vast collection of Marvel Comic's had become boring. Obviously, even Stan "The Man" hadn't tackled some problems. Primal groan, sorrowful moan and wounded words crashed to the floor. "Pleasseee!" Wasn't it bad enough she made me miss the horror flick *The Omen* the week before, now I had to miss Block Party Day too.

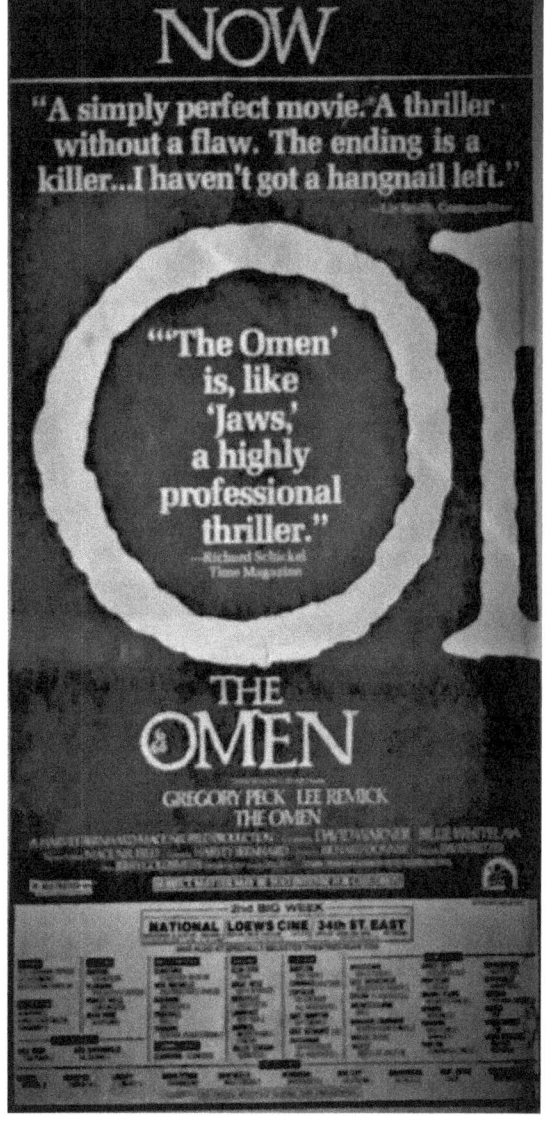

"You should have thought of that before you started living your life like a reckless lunatic," mom exaggerated, referring to the bicycle accident that caused my arm to break. "When the cops start bringing you home, it's the beginning of the end of innocence." I suppose she thought that last part sounded poetic, but to my ears, it was just stupid. The way mom acted, one would have thought she was an English teacher instead of just another Broadway bartender pouring drinks at the Oasis.

"It's not fair, it's not fair, it's not fair," I mumbled, pissed-off at a world. "Nobody else's mother put them on punishment and we were all together!"

"I'm not everybody's mother, I'm yours!" she screamed. "You're giving me a headache I really don't need right now. Please, not another word until I come out of this bathroom and I mean it. If you learn to act right, maybe I'll let you go out for a few hours, but for now I want to be left alone."

The moment mom slammed the bathroom door, as though on cue, I heard my cool clique's secret whistle screeching over the blare of the block. Without bothering to embarrass myself by looking out the window again, I knew the crew was straddled atop their sleek bikes as though they were huffing Harley hogs. Dressed in matching Pro-Keds, heavily starched Lee jeans and white t-shirts with scarlet gothic iron-on letters that read THE BOMB SQUAD, these dudes were my other family. We had all lived in the same pre-war building since we were small kids. We wasn't a fighting crew like the Savage Skulls or the Ballbusters, we just wanted to be known as rebellious graffiti gangsters who ruled the block from the black pleather thrones of our identical five-speed bikes.

"That fool must still be on lock-down," screamed Voodoo Ray, who sounded less Geechie than he had when he had first come-up from swamplands of Baton Rouge to the big city of dreams. Even after five years of battling the beast in the east, the boy still sounded more country than a jelly-jar full of moonshine.

"By the time Dorian can come outside we be fixin' to go back to school. Next year." As usual, it was Voodoo Ray who did the most jabber jawing. I suppose every crew needs a comedian for spontaneous snap sessions and dirty dozen debates, and Voodoo Ray was ours. While the crew cracked-up at Voodoo's pathetic jokes, souping him up like as if he was Richard Pryor, I retreated down the foyer to my secret fortress of solitude.

"To hell with Voodoo and the bike he rode in on," I mumbled.

Sneaking into grandma's onetime bedroom at the end of the hall, I stood in the doorway. In the corner was my mashed-up bike, an aluminum corpse that had once been my own cold-blooded Ross Apollo. With its twisted tires and bent handlebars, the broken bike had been the last birthday gift that had I gotten from grandma before she died. Crawling onto her now empty bed, I stared at the bike and quietly wept.

* * *

Two weeks before, when me and the crew finally finished our last class before summer vacation, we ran home as though we were prisoners who'd recently escaped our Catholic school jail. For the next two and a half months, there would no more nuns squashing fun or chain-smoking priests devouring guilty confessions. Instead, we looked forward to days of bliss, nights on the run (from the South Bronx to Harlem to Times Square, it was all about great adventures) and sneaking puffs of cheeba in the back staircase of our massive, marbled-wall building. It was the first summer we would all be turning thirteen and lord knows we already thought we were bad.

Rushing home as though the sweltering sun might soon eclipse out of pure spite, we pushed through our respective apartment doors, changed out of soiled school uniforms and grabbed our prized bikes. Minutes later the official members of the Bomb Squad were gathered in the crimson courtyard, shrieking like crazed ghetto wildcats.

Looking like the some kiddie version of the Hell's Angels, at least in our juvenile imaginations, we peddled fast and furious down the bustling Broadway streets, erupting with chocolate banshee laughter as annoyed pedestrians–ducking, dodging and sucking their teeth–screamed curses over our laughter. "Eat our dust!" we roared, sounding like a choir of badass hooligans in search of a trashy B-movie. Vaulting curbs, we tried not to spill as we headed for the eternal steepness of Dead Man's Hill.

Our sharp bikes were enhanced with lux-customized seats, silvery steel sissy bars like *Easy Rider* and small rainbow-hued plastic tubes spiked on each spinning spoke creating a whimsical kaleidoscope of bursting colors. Ranting and racing against time while trying not to bust my spastic behind, we skidded to the corner burning holes in the rubber soles of our Pro-Keds.

"Now what?" asked C.C., a hint of Nuyorican yellow rice and Goya beans in his sarcastic voice. Still, his love for all things graphic–be it the goofy hallucinations of Vaughn Bode, the pop art landscapes of Andy Warhol, the machine dreams Jack "The King" Kirby, the blackadelic mojo of Pedro Bell's madcap Funkadelic album covers or the thrilling blaxploitation movie posters hanging in the lobby of The Tapia Theater on a 147th—that inspired him with the lust to graffiti scrawl.

Before anyone bothered to answer, C.C. leapt from his bike, shaking a can of Red-Devil spray enamel. "Ya'll look out for the pigs," he barked, removing the plastic lid, but still not trying to do a bid for vandalizing public property. Approaching the reddish-brown brick wall as though it were the cracked ceiling in the Sistine Chapel, that streetwise Michelangelo had more passion in his crooked pinkie finger than most other writers had in their entire body.

While C.C. had never been St. Catherine's smartest student, he had been turned out by the freaky pyramid paradox of Egyptian hieroglyphics. History class wasn't a waste after all, he thought, coffee-colored eyes glued to the faded textbooks photos. "If King Tut were alive today, that black motherfucker would be bombing the system!" he yelled in the classroom, causing sadistic Sister Caron to flinch. Convinced that these followers of pharaoh had laid the foundation for the current generation of graff gangsters and aerosol outlaws, his head bopped to a James Brown beat that blared from a pimpmobile parked down the block.

"Hurry up with that shit," screamed Smokey, over the roar of Fred Wesley's flaming horn. "Fucking fuzz could be anywhere. I don't know 'bout you, but I ain't trying to get locked-up. My mom's ain't having it." Smokey was usually more irritable than the rest of us; perhaps it was this sullenness that caused a strange patch of whiteness to grow on top of his Afro.

As the aerosol flow of paint stained C.C.'s fingers a heavenly Empire Blue, all the compressed stress in his undiminished body seemed to disappear during the birth of artistic creation. C.C. escaped the harshness of his world, crazy daddy and helpless mom, through a colorful rabbit hole that led to a wonderland of animated visions. On the wall, stars exploded in the cosmos, disjointed letters morphed into Hanna-Barbara (Scooby Doo, Quick Draw McGraw, and Fred Flintstone) cartoon faces and naked big-breasted Bode broads.

Facing the wall as though in a trance, C.C.'s right hand did a tribal dance as we witnessed pure b-boy beauty developing before our fascinated eyes. Juggling spray cans like a mute court jester, C.C. switched colors (sunset orange, jungle green), intriguing a growing audience of neighborhood hood rats closely studying his style. Compared to C.C., we was nothing but toys, mere chums who just wanted to be down with the underground, still we didn't have the skills to pay the bills.

With a stylish elegance that blew our minds without even trying, his ten-minute masterpiece was beautiful. Adorned with shooting stars sailing over a towering atomic weapon on the verge of colorfully exploding; jeweled crowns floating over dripping abstract letters: *Introducing the Bomb Squad...C.C. 151.* Awestruck, we silently stared as though the dripping paint were the glimmering letters on a movie palace marquee, and the Bomb Squad were the latest bad boys riding into town. Super Fly suave and cooler than Iceberg Slim, we were lulled by the rhythm of the letters as though they were the sacred text of our personal street corner manifesto.

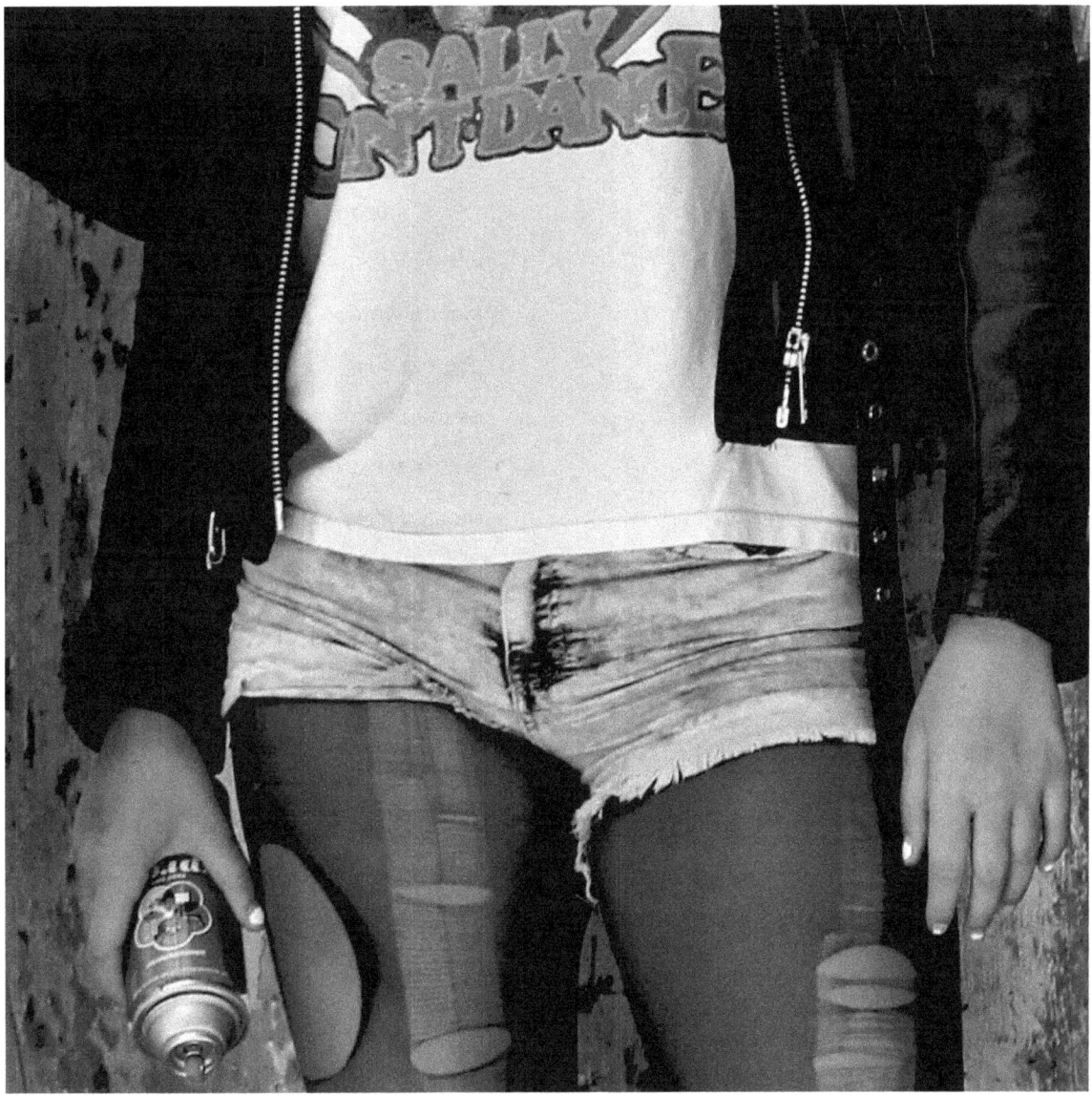

We were so into the creation of C.C.'s piece, we didn't notice when the men in blue rolled-up. Driving-up on the sidewalk as though they had watched too many reruns of Starsky and Hutch, their sickening siren blared. Screeching to a halt, a white middle-aged chubby cop rolled from the passenger side of a black and white ride.

"Stay where you are, ya black bastards!" he yelled. Wobbling like an overweight child, his thick Irish accent bubbled like stew, but those few words were our cue to mad-dash down that steep slope. C.C. swiftly tossed the empty paint cans over a near-by fence.

"Hope you thinkin' what I'm thinkin'," bellowed Voodoo, as the cocky cop crept closer. "it's Evel time, baby!" In our minds, the only white men that mattered were Burt Reynolds, Jesus Christ, Clint Eastwood and Evel Knievel. And while the Son of God might have died for our sins, it was damn hard to compete with a dude who mashed his bones simply for the thrill.

Racing down the hill, Smokey and C.C. were the undisputed leaders of the pack. Hunched over their handlebars they soared with the gracefulness of Joe Namath making another touchdown. "Hurry up you dumb shits!" whooped Smokey, before dipping around the corner.

Embracing more the stimulation of victory rather than the distress of defeat, C.C. rode the length of the hill on one wheel, popping prefect wheelies before soaring uptown on Riverside Drive. Oblivious to the honking horns while turning dangerous curves, C.C. vanished into traffic faster than Houdini.

Psyched on the natural high of Evel time, Voodoo Ray wasn't far behind. "You stop right this fucking minute," the cop's monstrous voice screamed. Briefly turning around to stare into his gruesome grill, I was definitely shaken. The mere thought of going to jail rocked my world. Suddenly, the pug-faced bastard tossed a crooked aluminum trashcan lid as though it were an oversized Frisbee.

Striking the Ross Apollo's rear wheel with the ultra adrenaline strength that only a doughnut eating pig could possess, the bicycle's front tire flipped as James Brown shrieked from a radio across the street. Outraged black folks shouted from car windows, smothering rage flaring in their eyes. Drenched in cold sweat, the salty drops dripped into my eyes and briefly blinded my great escape ride. "

Got ya little ass now," the cop yelled. Colliding head first into a mammoth mountain of garbage, I was dazed and confused. Landing squarely on my arm, I felt it snap like a dried-out wishbone. Without even looking, I knew my bike had also been trashed. If that cop had me cornered alone, my ass would have been grass. Grinning like an escaped mental patient over my shattered body, huffing and puffing as though he had been toking Cuban cigars since the age of two, the redheaded officer drooled.

"Get up!" he screamed, spitting spittle with each syllable. The cop's cold eyes had transformed into thin slits of fire as devilish thoughts fiddled like Nero inside his mind. Unloosing the solid oak nightstick from his side, he swung upward and I closed my eyes.

"Leave the boy alone," a strange voice drunkenly demanded. The gathering crowd murmured in agreement. Opening my eyes, I saw it was the neighborhood derelict Dres talking shit. Dressed in an unseasonably black corduroy suit, his sour sweat reeking of cheap sweet wine. Recklessly eyeballing the crazy cop through bloodshot sockets, he slurred, "He ain't even the one who was writing on the wall. "He just be the one who took da fall."

Surrounded by a grimacing jury of my peers, I was no longer scared. This motherfucker would have had to be badder than Shaft and Tarzan combined to whip my ass with all these beady-eyed witnesses lurking on Dead Man's Hill. "You must be the luckiest boy in this jungle," he whispered, pulling me to my feet. Without warning, he slapped my face. His steely hand against my cheek rattled my teeth like dice. Disgraced, disgusted and madder than hell, I limped over to my bike and cried like a newborn.

"Alright, let's break this up," screamed the other cop. Dragging me away by my broken arm as excruciating pain exploded in my shoulder.

"What you gonna do wit dat boy?" hollered Dres. "You better worry about what we gonna do to you?" the cop answered back. Still, the concerned crowd kept on following us until the moment the cops dropped me on my doorstep.

Hours later, after mom had brought me back from Harlem Hospital ("You're lucky all you only got was slapped!" she hollered), a grinning C.C. dragged my broken bike back to the crib.

"Dorian's really not supposed to be having any company," mom said sternly. Wearing fuzzy slippers, she had already poured herself a glass of white wine as the Fifth Dimension whined about "Aquarius" on the radio. "But, since you did drag that damn bike home I'll give you five minutes."

When C.C. walked into my junky bedroom littered with Marvel comics and slick Hot Wheel's tracks, I was still fuming. C.C. smiled, outlaw style from the corner of his mouth.

"Don't worry Dorian, 'cause this shit ain't over till it's over," he whispered, calming my nerves. "Those cops ain't got no idea that there's a revolution coming, an art revolution that got nothing to with museums and money. Us uptown heads 'bout to get busy, ya know, 'burn baby burn' and all that good shit." Pulling a red Pilot marker from his tattered jeans pocket C.C. tagged my ivory then-fresh cast: *The Bomb Squad Lives.*

Michael A. Gonzales writes about POP culture and books for Longreads, The Paris Review, CrimeReads, Catapult and Afro Punk. A Harlem native, his short fiction has appeared in The Root. com, Bronx Biannual edited by Miles Marshall Lewis, Brown Sugar edited by Carol Taylor and Black Pulp edited by Gary Phillips. Gonzales was never a graffiti writer, but, like his heroes Dondi and Lee, he always wanted to be.

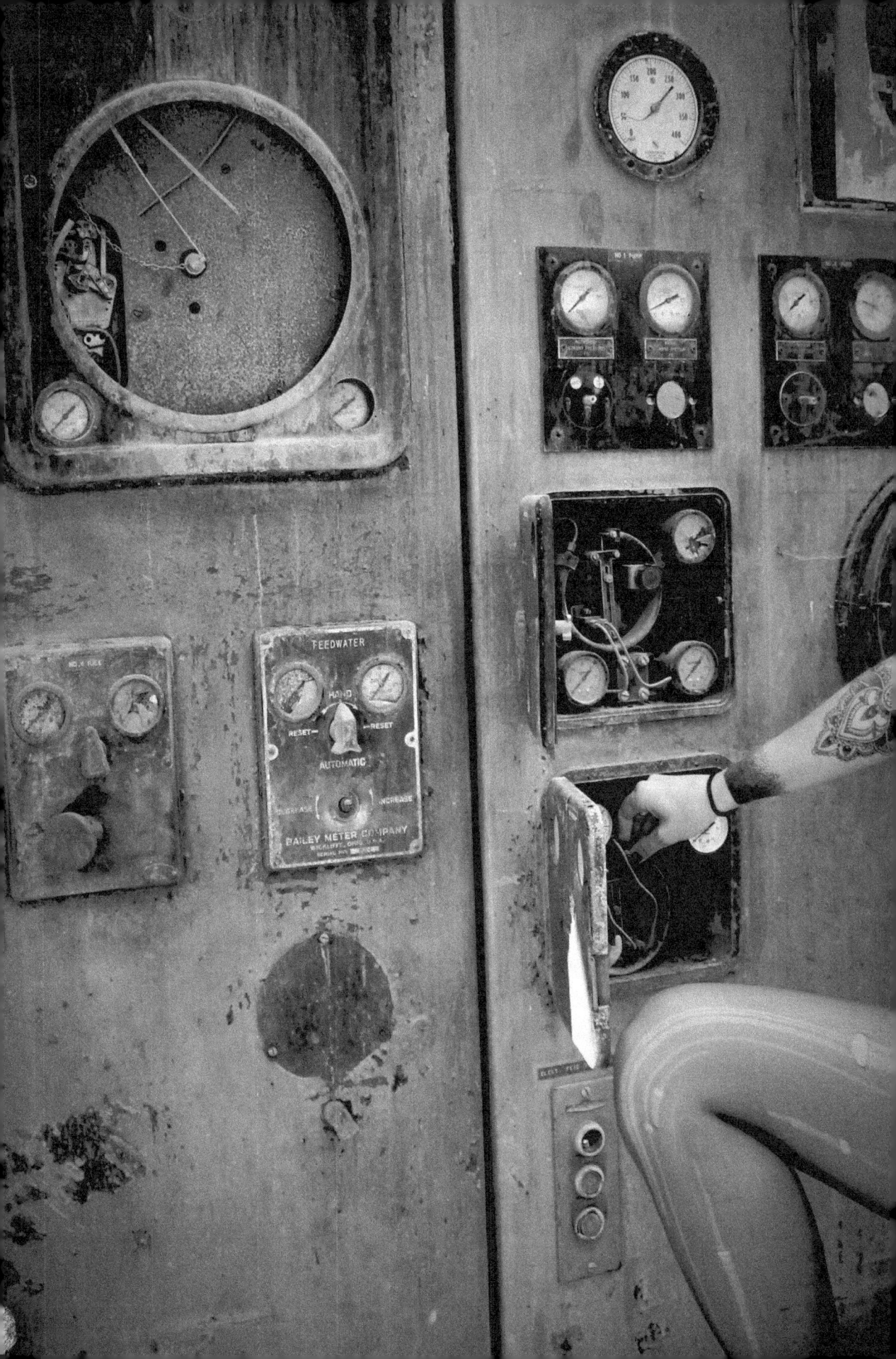

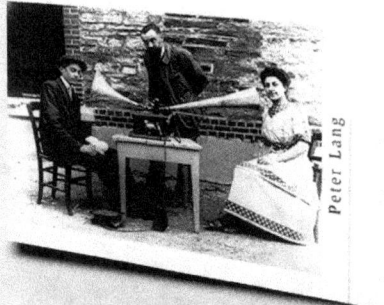

Modern French Identities

Michaël Abecassis avec Marcelline Block, Gudrun Ledegen et Maribel Peñalver Vicea (éds)

Le Grain de la voix dans le monde anglophone et francophone

Peter Lang

Michaël Abecassis · Marcelline Block · Gudrun Ledegen · Maribel Peñalver Vicea (éds)

Le Grain de la voix dans le monde anglophone et francophone

Oxford, 2019. XII, 332 pp., 28 fig. b/w, 6 tables
Modern French Identities. Vol. 130

pb.   ISBN 978-1-78874-107-1
CHF 70.– / €D 59.95 / €A 61.20 / £ 55.60 / £ 45.– / US-$ 67.95

eBook   ISBN 978-1-78874-108-8
CHF 70.– / €D 66.95 / €A 66.70 / £ 55.60 / £ 45.– / US-$ 67.95

Prix susceptibles de changements. Frais de port et d'emballage à charge du destinataire. CHF – PVC, comprend la TVA (valable pour la Suisse). €D – prix de vente fixe, comprend la TVA (valable pour l'Allemagne et les clients de l'UE sans N° TVA). €A – prix de vente fixe, comprend la TVA (valable pour l'Autriche). US-$/£/€ – PVC HT.

 Veuillez commander en ligne sous **www.peterlang.com**
Veuillez envoyer votre commande à **order@peterlang.com**

Nouvelle parution

Comme l'a noté le philosophe Jacques Derrida, l'enregistrement des voix a été l'un des évènements marquants du siècle passé. Le sociolinguiste William Labov s'est intéressé aux motivations sociales des variations phonologiques, mais non pas à la voix en tant que telle. Les recherches effectuées sur la texture et la qualité de la voix ou la relation entre la voix et l'affect sont beaucoup plus rares. Le sujet est mentionné dans les discussions sur la musique, le doublage, le théâtre et la traduction, sans toutefois être analysé en profondeur. Les articles sur la voix correspondent en outre à un développement relativement récent dans les domaines de la psycholinguistique et de la psychoacoustique, lié à un regain d'intérêt pour les études sur l'émotion de manière générale. Le présent recueil d'articles offre une perspective pluridisciplinaire au carrefour entre la sociolinguistique, la phonologie et les études cinématographiques.

 Abonnez-vous à nos newsletters
www.peterlang.com/subscribe

 Découvrez nos collections eBook
www.peterlang.com/ebooks

PETER LANG
ÉDITIONS SCIENTIFIQUES INTERNATIONALES

BERN · BERLIN · BRUXELLES · ISTANBUL
NEW YORK · OXFORD · WARSZAWA · WIEN

 /PeterLangPublishers

 /peterlanggroup

 /company/peterlangpublishers

Peter Lang AG, Wabernstrasse 40, 3007 Berne, Suisse

AN EXCERPT OF THE 2019 BOOK,

LE GRAIN DE LA VOIX DANS LE MONDE ANGLOPHONE ET FRANCOPHONE,

EDITED BY MICHAËL ABECASSIS, MARCELLINE BLOCK, GUDRUN LEDEGEN, AND MARIBEL PEÑALVER VICEA
(BERN, BERLIN, BRUXELLES, FRANKFURT AM MAIN, NEW YORK, OXFORD, WIEN: PETER LANG, MODERN FRENCH IDENTITIES, 2018).

WE GRATEFULLY ACKNOWLEDGE PETER LANG PUBLISHING FOR GRANTING PERMISSION TO PUBLISH THIS EXCERPT.
MICHAËL ABECASSIS, MARCELLINE BLOCK, GUDRUN LEDEGEN, AND MARIBEL PEÑALVER VICEA, EDS.,
LE GRAIN DE LA VOIX DANS LE MONDE ANGLOPHONE ET FRANCOPHONE
(BERN, BERLIN, BRUXELLES, FRANKFURT AM MAIN, NEW YORK, OXFORD, WIEN: PETER LANG, MODERN FRENCH IDENTITIES, 2019)
EXCERPT FROM THE VOICES PROJECT OF
LE GRAIN DE LA VOIX
DANS LE MONDE ANGLOPHONE ET FRANCOPHONE

The Project on French Voices offers more than 60 entries written by academics about the memorable voices of influential people in the francophone world. Each entry—whether about an actor/actress, a singer, a journalist or a politician—describes the particular features that made these voices so distinctive and important. The voice is in itself a great source of information, as Bailblé puts it:

> De l'être du sujet : sexe, âge, identité : origine socio-culturelle et empreinte vocale particulière (voice print) ; typage (façon de poser la voix, accents, habitudes articulatoires) mais aussi timbre de voix personnelle. [1]
> [About the being of the subject: sex, age, identity: socio-cultural origin and particular voice print; typing (way of posing the voice, accents, articulatory habits) but also the personal timbre of one's voice.]

The voice is not only the means through which a person expresses himself/herself, but also, it is an entity that exists on its own in our collective memory.

---

[1]   Claude Bailblé, «Programmation de l'écoute 3», *Cahiers du cinéma* 297 (février 1979): 53.

Charles Aznavour (1924-2018)

By Marcelline Block

On October 1, 2018, the world lost one of the most legendary figures in entertainment when Charles Aznavour—whose career as a singer, songwriter, and actor was eight-decades-long— passed away at age 94 from cardiac arrest. Dubbed France's "little 'giant'"[2] due to his diminutive stature which belied his artistic greatness, Aznavour had just toured in Japan in September 2018.

Aznavour's passing plunged France into a period of national mourning. At the state funeral held for him at Les Invalides in Paris, Aznavour was eulogized by French President Emmanuel Macron as well as Armenian Prime Minister Nikol Pashinyan. Aznavour was born in Paris on May 24, 1924 to an Armenian immigrant family, and was given Armenian citizenship in 2008. In discussing how his Armenian heritage influenced his career as a French-born singer-songwriter, Aznavour stated that, "'I have an Eastern voice and a Western way of writing songs.'"[3]

Although he had been performing since childhood, as a young adult, Aznavour was discovered and launched by Edith Piaf. Aznavour possessed one of the most recognizable and iconic French singing voices of all time. As Alan Riding notes, Aznavour's "highly distinct tenor voice, with its raspy nasal color, had a Mediterranean quality that appealed to a variety of audiences."[4] Aznavour's "voice like caramel"[5] could be heard in his classic chansons such as "Tu t'Laisses Aller," "She," "La Bohème" and "Les Deux guitares." He performed at sold-out concerts at Carnegie Hall and the Royal Albert Hall, among other prestigious international venues, holding concerts all over the world up until his death, and had a

European tour scheduled to begin in November 2018. Sadly, this tour would never take place.

Along with his songs, Aznavour's distinctive voice could also be heard when he performed roles in more than 60 films—including as the titular character of François Truffaut's New Wave classic, *Tirez sur le pianiste / Shoot the Piano Player* (1960)—for which he was awarded the César d'honneur in 1997.

Sometimes labelled the "French Frank Sinatra," Aznavour, as a singer and songwriter of over 1000 songs and of records that sold nearly 200 million copies, impacted and influenced the music industry in France for generations. His legacy for French music history and culture is undeniable; after all, "Aznavour poured out tales in songs that helped define the French chanson."[6]

Yet Aznavour's renown transcended the French language—he often sang in languages other than French (including Armenian as well as English, Italian and Spanish)—and his natal France, such as when CNN named him "Entertainer of the Century" in 1998 and when he received a star on the Hollywood Walk of Fame in 2017. He was especially recognized in his parents' native Armenia, for which he was a tireless advocate and philanthropist, including commemorating the Armenian genocide with his song "Ils sont tombés" and supporting the country after its 1988 earthquake through his charitable foundation for Armenia. In 2009, Aznavour was appointed Armenian Ambassador to Switzerland as well as permanent representative of Armenia to the United Nations in Geneva.

I feel fortunate to have attended Aznavour's "farewell concert" in New York City's Madison Square Garden in September 2014 (to which he would return to

2   Fiachra Gibbons, "France Bids Farewell to Singer Aznavour, its Little 'Giant,'" *Jakarta Post*, October 5, 2018, http://www.thejakartapost.com/life/2018/10/05/france-bids-farewell-to-singer-aznavour-its-little-giant.html.

3   Anastasia Tsioulcas, « The Voice of France, Charles Aznavour, Dies at 94, » *NPR Music*, October 1, 2018, https://www.npr.org/2018/10/01/653285165/the-voice-of-france-charles-aznavour-dies-at-94.

4   Alan Riding, "Aznavour, the Last Chanteur," *New York Times*, October 18, 1998, https://www.nytimes.com/1998/10/18/arts/music-aznavour-the-last-chanteur.html.

5   Tsioulcas, "The Voice of France."

6   Ibid.

perform again in 2016). It was a joy and a privilege to witness as well as experience Aznavour's powerful, soulful and dynamic onstage presence—even at age 90—as well as the deep emotional connection between Aznavour and his public as the multigenerational, multilingual audience eagerly implored him for encores and to sing in a variety of languages, to which he gladly obliged.

After the state funeral ceremony at Les Invalides, as Aznavour's coffin was led away for private burial in Montfort-l'Amaury, his song "Emmenez-moi" was played. This song's refrain, "emmenez-moi au bout de la terre / emmenez-moi au pays des merveilles" serves as a fitting commemoration and tribute to Azanvour, whose death signifies the loss of "the voice of France."[7]

Gaston Bachelard (1884-1962)

By Michaël Abecassis, the University of Oxford
(Translated from the French by Marcelline Block)

The philosopher Gaston Bachelard was born in the small village of Bar-sur-Aube in Champagne-Ardenne. The rare video recordings of him that remain—those of an old man with a bushy white beard, sitting in the middle of piles of books—have made him the archetypal philosopher in the collective imagination. Listening to his unusual gravelly voice, marked by a pronounced Burgundy accent replete with the rolling "r," evokes a surreal quality that nurtured the collective imagination; in this sense, it is in itself an invitation to dream.

Sidonie-Gabrielle Colette (1873-1954)

By Michaël Abecassis, The University of Oxford

(Translated from the French by Marcelline Block)

Sidonie-Gabrielle Colette was born in the family birthplace of Saint-Sauveur-en-Puisaye, a village in Bourgogne. She possessed the husky, gravelly voice of a peasant, rolling the Burgundian "r," as evidenced by the rare recordings that remain of her voice. Louis Aragon associates this voice with the Bourgogne wine terroir in a poem that he wrote the day after her death: "with all the varietals of a Beaune/The rolling of the 'r' like a bottle of wine in the cellar."

Jean D'Ormesson (1925-2018)

By Michaël Abecassis, The University of Oxford

Jean D'Ormesson was above all a voice and a presence emanating from every television set. Born to an haute bourgeois Parisian family as Count Jean Bruno Wladimir Francois-de-Paule Lefèvre, he was elected to the Académie Française in 1970. An exceptional orator, with sparkling blue eyes and a benevolent smile playing on his lips, he elegantly wielded the passé simple and the imperfect subjunctive. He spoke eloquently and with an affectation in his voice that seemed charmingly old-fashioned, as if it belonged to another era. Despite what he said, describing himself jocularly as "ringard" (out of fashion)[8], his persistently young and dynamic wit was very much in line with his times. These conversations had something of a timeless quality. Addressing himself to imaginary interlocutors, he brought to his conversations the greatest names in literature, a joyous erudition that left no spectator indifferent.

7   Ibid.

8   Jean-Claude Vantroyen, "Jean d'Ormesson au «Soir» en 2016 : «Je suis un ringard qu'on applaudit»," *Le Soir*, 29 January 2016, http://plus.lesoir.be/23527/article/2016-01-29/jean-dormesson-au-soir-en-2016-je-suis-un-ringard-quon-applaudit#.

Francis Lai (1932-2018)

By Marcelline Block

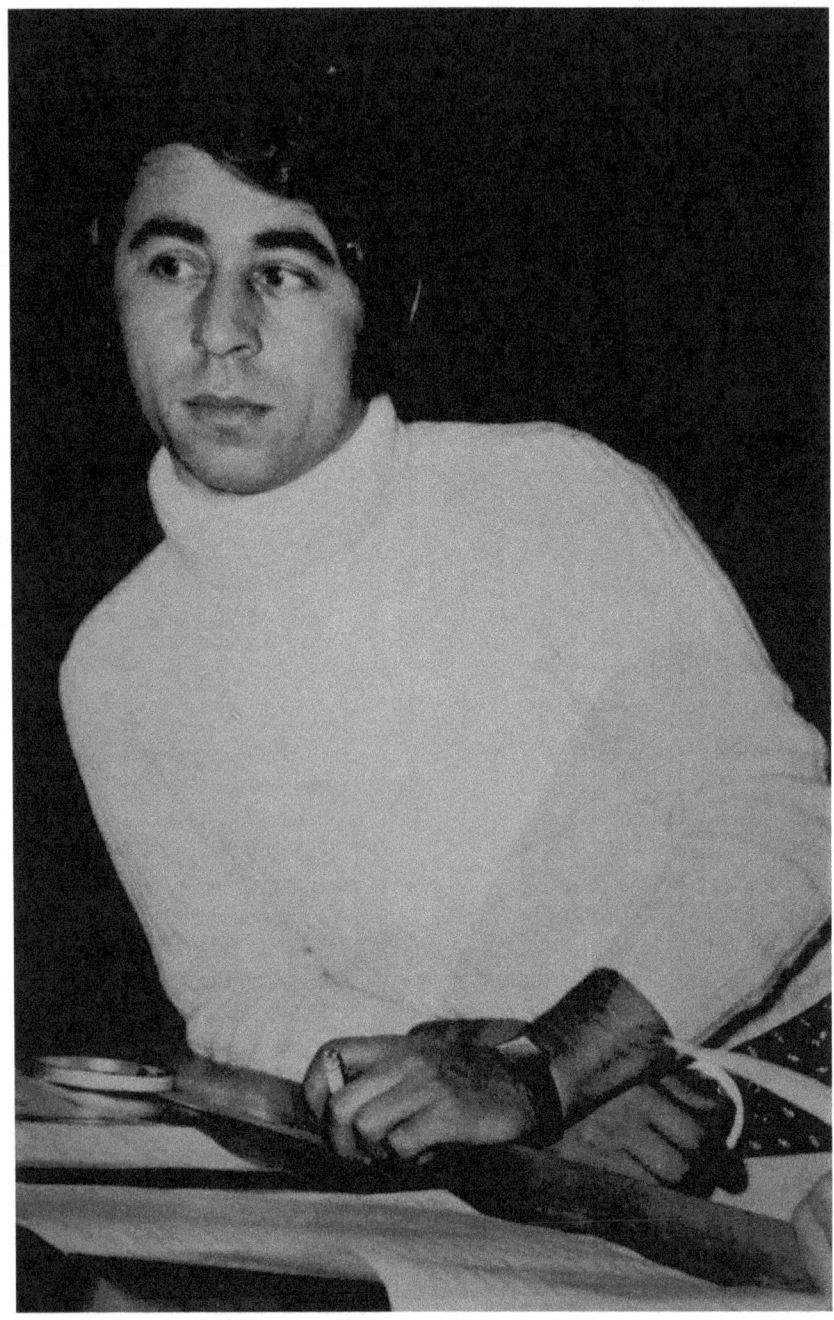

In the spring of 2017, I interviewed Academy Award-winning French film score composer Francis Lai about his work with actress Sylvia Kristel (1952-2012) for the film *Emmanuelle II* (Francis Giacobetti, 1975) in which Kristel starred as the titular character. Lai composed the score for *Emmanuelle II*, including writing the music for the film's haunting, romantic ballad "L'amour d'aimer" (lyrics by Leo Carrier and Catherine Desage). "L'amour d'aimer" is sung by Kristel in a type of duo with Lai, whose voice can also be heard in this song.

As he was born in Nice, Lai's voice—which radiated energy and his youthful attitude—betrayed a slight *accent niçois*. His voice had hardly changed in the nearly fifty years since he gave his brief, heartfelt Oscar acceptance speech in 1971 at age 38 when he received the Academy Award for Best Original Score for the American melodrama *Love Story* (Arthur Hiller, 1970), filmed on the grounds of Harvard University.

When Lai spoke during our interview, his words were punctuated by occasional peals of laughter, such as when he related how, due to his phobia of planes, he nearly did not compose the score for *Love Story*, since it was necessary for him to fly to the United States to do so. Therefore, *Love Story*'s producer flew to Paris to convince Lai to compose the film's score by screening the film for him. Upon viewing it, Lai was immediately taken with *Love Story* and accepted to write the music for it, for which he ultimately won both the Golden Globe and the Oscar for Best Original Score.

Lai was a prolific composer who wrote scores for over 100 films. At the time that I interviewed Lai in May 2017, he was in the midst of composing the music for Claude Lelouch's then current film project, *Chacun sa vie/Everyone's Life* (2017), which features Johnny Hallyday—another iconic French voice—in his final film performance. Indeed, Lai's decades-long collaboration with Lelouch was fruitful and brought Lai renown as a film composer. Lai composed his first film score for Lelouch's Academy Award-winning *Un homme et une femme* (1966), for which Lai was nominated for the Golden Globe for Best Original Score. Nearly five decades later, Lai wrote what would ultimately become his last film score for Lelouch's forthcoming *Les plus belles années* (2019). This film stars Anouk Aimée and Jean-Louis Trintignant, who previously portrayed the titular couple in *Un homme et un femme* over fifty years ago. Thus, Lai's career in film music came full circle, as it began and concluded with Lelouch's films starring these two actors, since on November 7, 2018, Francis Lai left us at age 86.

Lai's lengthy life and career in the music industry, and his major contributions to the history and culture of French as well as US film form a long-lasting legacy for the arts that will never be forgotten. I am most grateful to have been in conversation with Francis Lai and to have been able to interview him. Conversing with him was a pleasure, as was hearing his voice, which emanated kindness, positivity, and youthfulness—it did not betray his age. He shared much insight with me about his creative process for composing film music and expressed his lifelong passion for his vocation, as demonstrated by his numerous current and upcoming projects at the time of our interview. In particular, I will never forget when we discussed his total dedication to composing the music for *Love Story*, which has particular personal resonance and meaning for me as a Harvard College alumna. Francis Lai was delighted when I told him about the annual Harvard tradition of screening *Love Story* for the entering class of first-year undergraduates at the start of every academic year.

I will always treasure my conversations with Francis Lai, and greatly look forward to the publication of my interview with him in Jeremy Richey's forthcoming book entitled *A Return to Utrecht: The Sylvia Kristel Archives*. Lai's voice exuded his lifelong enthusiasm and passion for music, as well as his belief that "music is the only universal language that can cross all boundaries. We don't need to speak the language, only the music. Music carries our profound sentiments, and if it can make life easier, if it can bring a smile to someone's face, if it can bring us joy, I think that's the goal of music."[9] Although sadly Francis Lai is no longer with us, his music, his voice, and his legacy will endure far beyond his lifetime.

Jean-Pierre Marielle (1932-): "A voice that is 'reconnaissable entre mille' "

By Marcelline Block

Throughout his successful career on stage and screen spanning more than six decades, with appearances in over 100 films, Jean-Pierre Marielle's signature as an actor is his unmistakable voice — with its deep, rich and resonant velvety timbre — which, when he made his onscreen debut in the 1950s, allowed him to incarnate characters who were more advanced in age than him. Whether in Bertrand Tavernier's *Coup de Torchon* (1981), Alain Corneau's *Tous les matins du monde* (1991), Chantal Akerman's *Demain* on *déménage* (2004), or Jean-Pierre Jeunet's *Micmacs à tire-larigot* (2009), Marielle

9   Francis Lai interviewed by Marcelline Block, May 2017, for Jeremy Richey's forthcoming book, *From Emmanuelle to Chabrol: Sylvia Kristel in the Seventies*. Transcribed and translated from French to English by Marcelline Block.

has made his mark onscreen with his inimitable voice, which has been labelled "reconnaissable entre mille"[10] such as those of Michel Bouquet and Louis Jouvet. Marielle's instantly recognizable voice was heard in a radio advertisement for Père Magloire Calvados, which aired on RTL and Europe 1 in December 2013. He also lent his voice to films including the French versions of the BBC production *Pride* (John Downer, 2004) and Pixar's beloved *Ratatouille* (Brad Bird/Jan Pinkava, 2007) as well as *L'Apprenti Père Noël* (Luc Vinciguerra, 2010) and *Phantom Boy* (Jean-Loup Felicioli/Alain Gagnol, 2015). Beyond radio, film, and theatre, however, perhaps the best way to truly appreciate, enjoy, and fully experience the unforgettable quality of Marielle's iconic voice is to listen to him reading his own words in the audiobook version of his autobiography, *Le Grand n'importe quoi* (Paris: Éditions Calmann-Lévy, 2010), in which he discusses, among other topics, his passion for jazz.

Henri Salvador (1917-2008)

By Marcelline Block

Iconic French singer and songwriter Henri Salvador's influence was felt across continents and encompassed numerous musical and performative genres as well as venues. Among his honors and awards from France are the Legion of Honor and National Order of Merit.

Salvador—a "velvet-voiced, Nat King Cole-like crooner and jazz guitarist"[11]—was born in Cayenne, French Guiana in 1917; his family moved to Paris during his childhood. This is where Salvador encountered jazz and taught himself to play the guitar, embarking upon his career in music while he was still an adolescent by performing in concert halls in Paris.

Salvador performed not only on stage—at famed Parisian theatres and music halls such as the Alhambra, ABC, and Bobino—but also in film and particularly on television during the 1960s and 70s. Furthermore, Salvador is credited, alongside his frequent song writing collaborator Boris Vian (1920-1959) with bringing rock n' roll to France in the 1950s. In addition, Salvador was influential upon Latin American and Brazilian music, especially the Bossa Nova.

Salvador has been described as possessing a "silken" and "honeyed" voice; of his voice, Salvador himself stated that, "'I don't sing, I whisper….When you whisper into the mike, you are able to transmit real feeling.'"[12] Indeed, this is demonstrated by the fact that Salvador "was adored by an immense public, and especially by the young. It was natural, his songs were sensitive and delicate. He sang….with a tender, caressing, melancholy voice – he expressed better than anyone the essence of that generation."[13] These qualities of Salvador's voice come through beautifully in his iconic children's song "Une Chanson douce" (1950; lyrics by Maurice Pon).

Salvador's well-known penchant for exuberant laughter led to his nickname "Monsieur Joie-de-Vivre."[14] In Quincy Jones' estimation, "With Henri I've learnt that a big laugh is a really loud noise from the soul saying, 'Ain't that the truth?'"[15]

Salvador died in early February 2008 at age 90, a few months after giving his farewell concert in December 2007 at Le Palais des Congrès in Paris.

10   Bernard Loupias, "L'abécédaire de Jean-Pierre Marielle," *Le Nouvel observateur*, 17 September 2010, http://bibliobs.nouvelobs.com/documents/20100916.BIB5640/l-039-abecedaire-de-jean-pierre-marielle.html.

11   Pierre Perrone, "Henri Salvador: France's 'Monsieur Joie de Vivre,'" *The Independent*, February 14, 2008, https://www.independent.co.uk/news/obituaries/henri-salvador-frances-monsieur-joie-de-vivre-781981.html.

12   Ibid.

13   Patrick O'Connor, "Obituary: Henri Salvador," *The Guardian*, February 18, 2008, https://www.theguardian.com/music/2008/feb/18/obituaries.france.

14   Peter Culshaw, "Seduced by Monsieur Joie-de-Vivre," *The Telegraph*, March 24, 2007, https://www.telegraph.co.uk/culture/music/rockandjazzmusic/3663970/Seduced-by-Monsieur-Joie-de-Vivre.html.

15   Ibid.

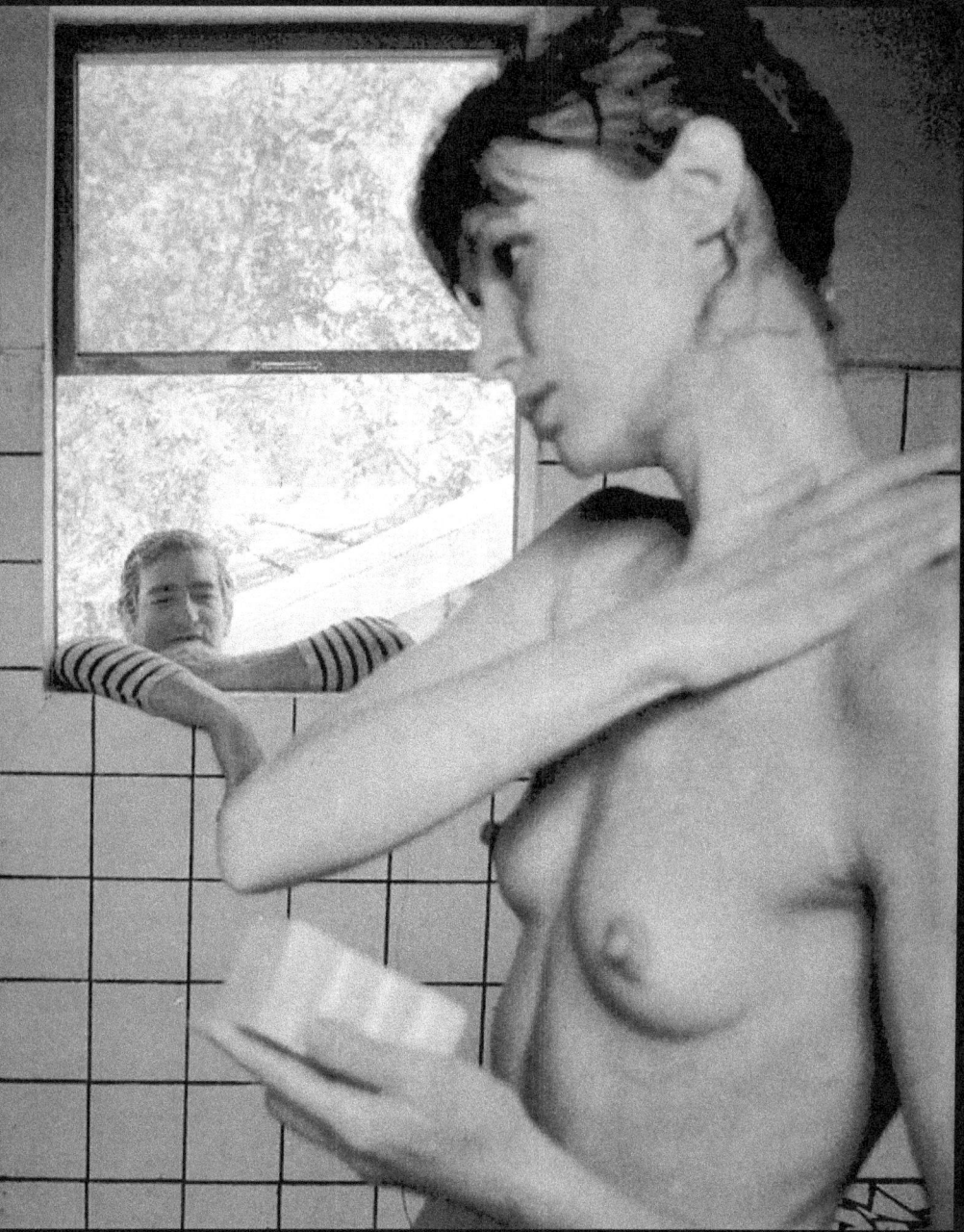

Adolphe Viezzi & Henri Lassa
présentent

un film de BERTRAND TAVERNIER

COUP DE TORCHON

écrit par Jean Aurenche et Bertrand Tavernier
d'après le roman de Jim Thompson "POP 1280"

avec

Philippe NOIRET / Isabelle HUPPERT / Jean-Pierre MARIELLE

Stéphane AUDRAN / Guy MARCHAND / Eddy MITCHELL / Irène SKOBLINE

une co-production les films de la tour - film A2 - little bear

OUT OF THE DARKNESS AND INTO THE LIGHT:

A TRIBUTE TO JOE D'AMATO

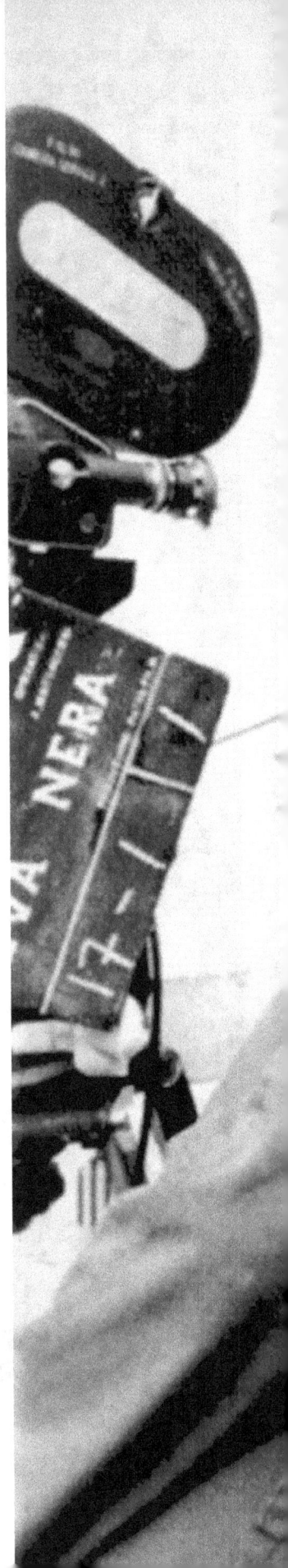

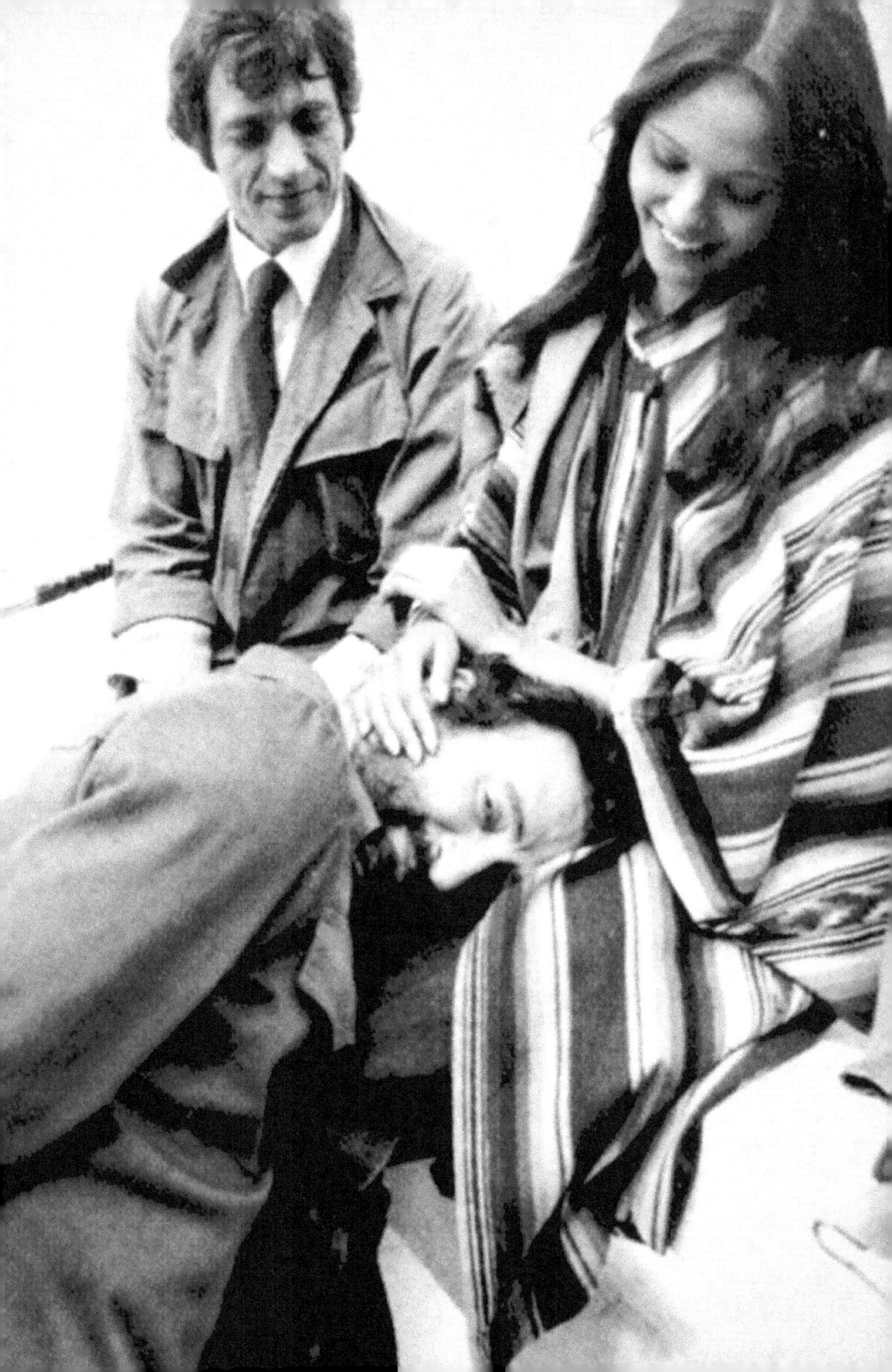

IT'S HARD TO BELIEVE BUT IT'S BEEN TWENTY YEARS
SINCE WE LOST THE LEGENDARY
ARISTIDE MASSACCESI,
ONE OF THE MOST MISUNDERSTOOD AND VISIONARY
ITALIAN FILMMAKERS OF ALL TIME.

MASSACCESI OR, AS HE IS BETTER KNOWN TO HIS FANS,
JOE D'AMATO
BEGAN WORKING IN THE ITALIAN FILM INDUSTRY IN THE FIFTIES BEFORE BECOMING ONE OF
THE MOST CREATIVE AND IN DEMAND CAMERA OPERATORS OF THE SIXTIES.
D'AMATO LEARNED HIS CRAFT THROUGHOUT THE SIXTIES BY WORKING WITH EVERYONE
FROM MARIO BAVA TO JEAN-LUC GODARD AND BY THE DAWN OF THE SEVENTIES HE
TRANSITIONED FIRST TO CINEMATOGRAPHER TO FINALLY DIRECTOR.
BETWEEN 1972 AND 1999, D'AMATO WOULD SERVE AS DIRECTOR, AND USUALLY
CINEMATOGRAPHER, ON A WHOPPING NEAR 200 FILMS, ALL OF WHICH WOULD BEAR HIS
VERY DISTINCTIVE AND OFTEN CONTROVERSIAL STAMP.
THERE WOULD BE NO GENRE THAT D'AMATO WAS AFRAID TO TOUCH FROM INSANELY
GORY HORROR FILMS TO PERIOD-PIECE HARDCORE WORKS.
LIKE GODARD HE WOULD OFTEN REFER TO HIMSELF AS JUST A BUSINESSMAN THROUGHOUT
HIS CAREER BUT ALSO, LIKE THE ICONIC FRENCH PROVOCATEUR, HE WOULD NEVER
BETRAY WHAT HE TRULY WAS, A GREAT AND RESTLESS ARTIST WHO DIDN'T UNDERSTAND
THE WORD COMPROMISE.

OFTEN UNFAIRLY MALIGNED AS SECOND-TIERED TO THE LIKES OF DARIO ARGENTO AND
LUCIO FULCI IN THE CULT FILM COMMUNITY, D'AMATO'S LEGACY HAS BEEN UNDERGOING
A MAJOR AND MUCH NEEDED REAPPRAISAL IN THE PAST FEW YEARS THANKS TO SEVERAL
COMPREHENSIVE SPECIAL EDITION REISSUES OF SOME OF HIS KEY WORKS.
TO CELEBRATE D'AMATO'S CAREER AND LEGACY ON THE 20TH ANNIVERSARY OF HIS
PASSING, I HAVE INVITED FILM HISTORIAN SAMM DEIGHAN AND ARTIST JUSTIN COFFEE TO
SHARE SOME OF THEIR THOUGHTS ON JOE AND TALK ABOUT THEIR CONTRIBUTIONS TO
SOME OF THESE SPECTACULAR BLU-RAY SPECIAL EDITIONS.

THANKS SO MUCH TO SAMM AND JUSTIN FOR THEIR TIME AND THANKS SO MUCH TO MY
FELLOW FANS WHO HAVE HELPED KEEP JOE D'AMATO'S ASTOUNDING CINEMATIC LEGACY
VERY MUCH ALIVE DESPITE THE CONCENTRATED EFFORT BY MANY TO
WRITE HIM OUT OF FILM HISTORY.

AD OGNI SANTO VIEN SUA FESTA!

JEREMY R RICHEY

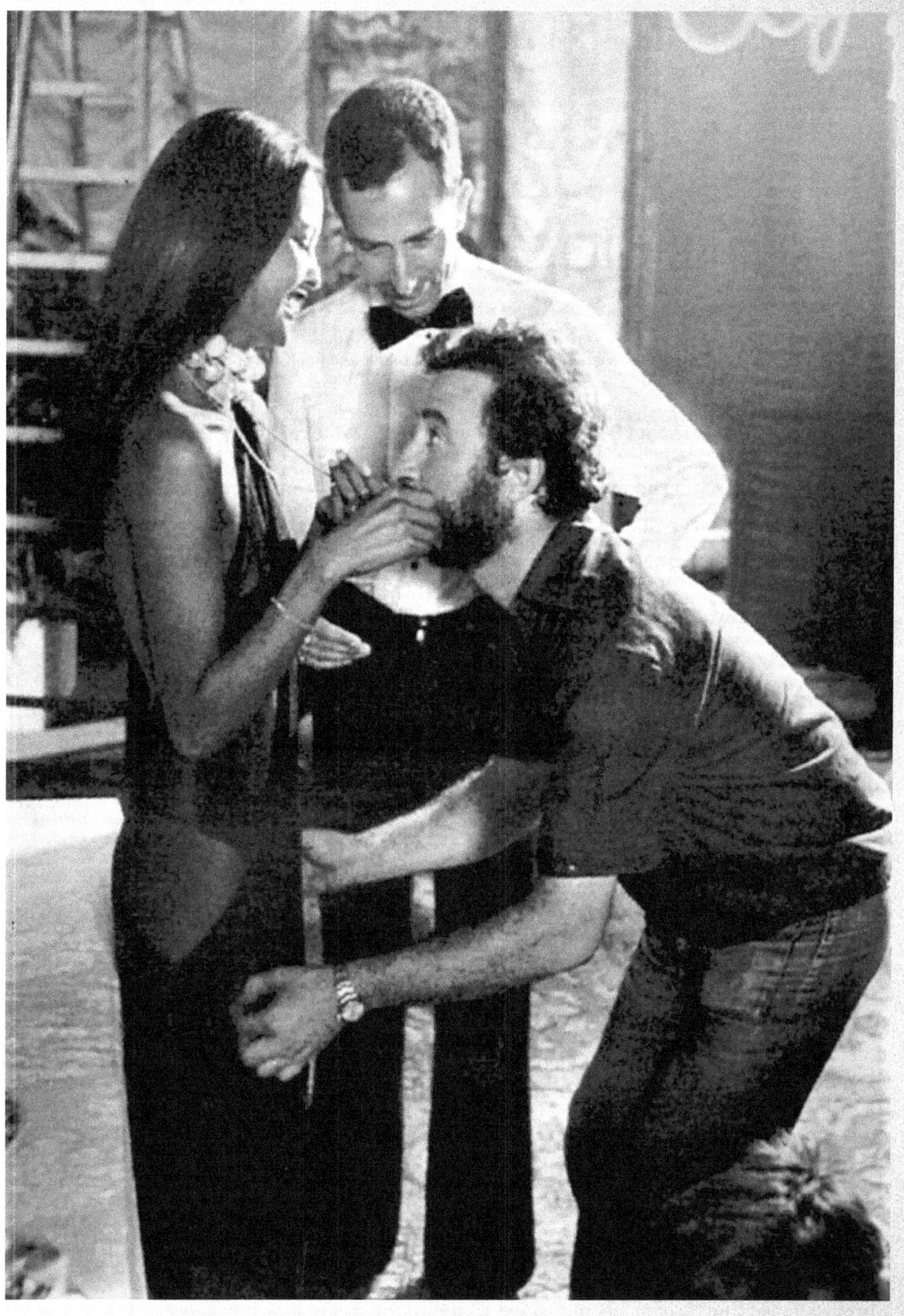

"""ABOVE, AND PRECEDING PAGE, D'AMATO WITH HIS FREQUENT COLLABORATOR LAURA GEMSER"""

AN INTERVIEW WITH

SAMM DEIGHAN

BY JEREMY R RICHEY

JR: Hey Samm, thanks so much for agreeing to take some time to discuss our shared love of Aristide Massaccesi (Joe D'Amato) and his work. As I stated in my intro, Joe wore a lot of different hats behind the camera throughout his decades long career as initially a cinematographer, then director and finally as pornographer and he has very passionate fans of all three of those roles. Which aspect of D'Amato's career are you most fond of?

SD: I don't know if I draw a real distinction between "director" and "pornographer." One of the things I love so much about D'Amato is that he covered a wide range of genres, and like other Eurocult directors such as Jess Franco and Jean Rollin, was also willing to explore sex films. I'm a person who is easily bored and with all three of those directors, discovering their work has always been so exciting because you never know exactly what you're going to get (in terms of genre, violence, sexual content, etc). And as for which hat I think D'Amato wore best, I'd have to say director. He made films that no one else could have made: because they were bold and imaginative in their treatment of sex, violence, and genre films, and maybe just because many of them are totally off the wall in a way that I find really exciting. This continued all the way from the beginning of his directorial career towards its conclusion. It frustrates me so much that people talk about him like he's some kind of unworthy schlockmeister. It makes me feel like anyone saying that hasn't seen more than one or two of his films.

How did you first discover D'Amato and what were your initial thoughts towards him and his work?

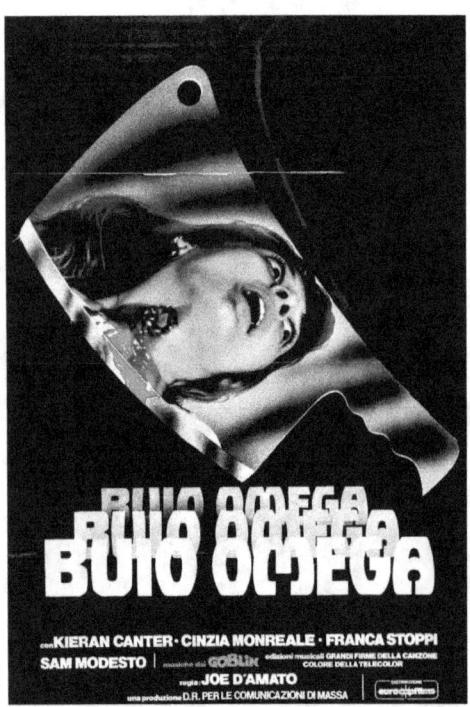

I want to say that the first film I discovered—or at least the first film I consciously knew to be D'Amato's work—was *Buio Omega* (1979). From the beginning of my teenage obsession with cult cinema, I've sought out necrophilia movie and, to me, this is the Holy Grail of them all. It might not be the most obscure, it might not be as emotionally affecting as something like *Nekromantik* (1987), but it's the best.

Based on my obsession with that film, I sought out his gore films with actor/writer George Eastman soon after and was astounded to learn (when I was about 16) that someone combined hardcore pornography with the horror genre. It was a revelation. And I know I saw *Ator, the Fighting Eagle* (1982) around that time too (I have an abiding love for '80s sword and sorcery films), but I don't think I realized it was D'Amato. If you're someone with a voracious appetite for Italian cult cinema, chances are he's snuck in there at least once or twice without you having any idea.

While D'Amato has a dedicated cult following he hasn't found the more mainstream acceptance of more usually celebrated figures in Italian genre cinema like Bava, Argento or even Fulci. Why do you think this is?

I think there are three primary reasons. First is the availability of his films. I know that 20 years ago, when I started really getting into cult cinema, his work was very difficult to get ahold of and there are still many films of his without proper releases. Second is word of mouth. In the pre-internet days (or even early internet days), you only learned about directors through other fans, through books, and through people selling bootlegs. You had to pick carefully and I think it was often just easier to get into the work of a director that came highly recommended from other fans (like Argento). The third reason—and maybe the most serious—is the accessibility of his films (in terms of content). They're not for everyone and they certainly represent a specific kind of taste, even among extreme horror fans. I think some people can't handle at the low budgets, some people are made very uncomfortable by the use of sex or pornography, and so on. To me that inaccessibility just makes his work more magical.

With that in mind, what aspects of D'Amato's films do you think distinguishes him from his peers?

Well, I think the Italian cult directors who made—or sometimes made—horror films fell into a particular trap if they didn't make giallo films. For whatever reason, the giallo directors have always been the most popular, at least in terms of Italian cult cinema. I love the subgenre, but I don't really understand why this is. Maybe because those films follow a particular pattern that is easy to familiarize yourself with: you know what you're getting and once you've seen a few giallo films, there aren't a ton of surprises. But directors like Renato Polselli, D'Amato, and even Fulci are… different. They weren't interesting into sticking too closely to a particular formula or pattern. As I said above, I think that made D'Amato a lot more difficult to market and less accessible. D'Amato seemed to not care about that formula whatsoever and, again a lot like Fulci, his films have a rebellious, renegade quality.

Throughout his career D'Amato directed films throughout a number of genres including horror, comedy, period pieces and erotic films. What type do you think he excelled in the best?

I think he excelled at making films about the utter vileness of human nature: whether that's horror, exploitation, or erotica. To me, that's one of the unifying traits of his films across genre, but I think it often works the best in his exploitation films like *Emmanuelle's Revenge* (1975). Not that I don't love his horror films, but what I love about them is not that they're scary or gory, or that they make use of particular genre tropes, but that they are about truly awful people being awful to each other (as in *Buio Omega* or even *Death Smiles on a Murderer*).

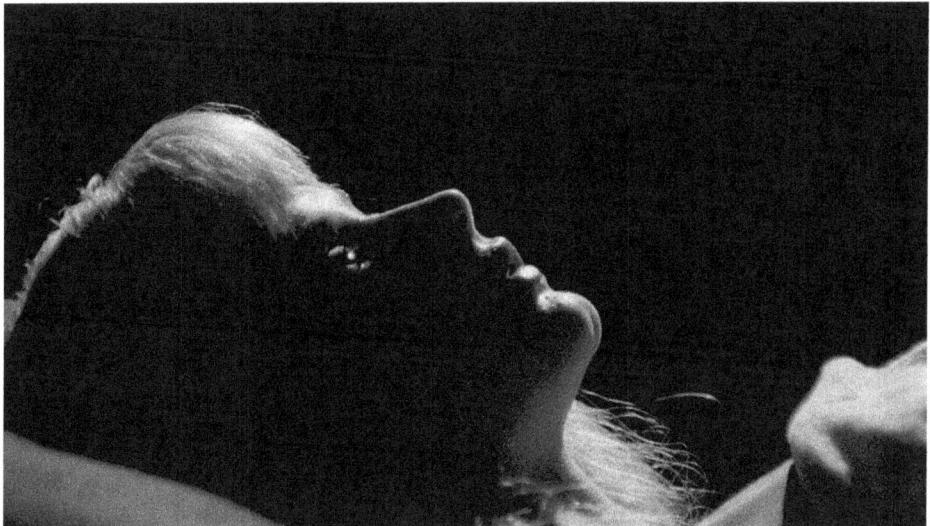

Death Smiles on a Murderer is one of the most striking debuts of the seventies but, thanks to Arrow's Blu-ray special edition, has perhaps only recently finally started to get its due. What are your thoughts on the film?

Honestly, I love it so much. It's one that I didn't see until later because it was so hard to find. No one talked about it, so it didn't even occur to me to think of it as an important title in his career that I should make an effort to seek out. I also think it's an important piece of evidence that he could make so much more than porn or gore films: it's a really effective, unsettling gothic thriller. Like Sergio Martino's *Your Vice is a Locked Room and Only I Have the Key* (1972), it pretends to be a giallo at points, but is really something much weirder. I don't know where to rank it in his filmography—if it should be a starting point for new fans or not—but at minimum anyone who likes Klaus Kinski needs to get on it immediately.

Despite working in a vast number of genres, D'Amato had a number of performers that he worked with regularly throughout the years. Who are some of your favorites that appeared?

I love Laura Gemser as much as everyone else, but for me there can be only one: Luigi Montefiori aka George Eastman. Tall, dark, and looking like he wants to absolutely murder you, he's one of my favorite actors from the period—and one of my favorite cult cinema figures in general, as he was also a pretty prolific writer. This is probably old news to most D'Amato fans, but Eastman wrote dozens of films, made-for-TV movies, and television series. Delightfully, he and D'Amato collaborated often and he wrote some of the particularly nasty D'Amato films he starred in. Like Christopher Lee, he was really too tall to be a romantic lead—he was 6'9'!!! so take a minute to think about how Mario Bava squeezed him in the back of that teensy car for *Rabid Dogs*—but has had such a versatile career as an actor because of his handsomeness and charisma, as well as his willingness to play monsters and really horrific characters.

D'Amato's films featured the scores of a some of the best composers of the period. What are your favorite scores?

I really love Goblin's moody score for *Buio Omega*, which is unlike anything else they've done (that I've heard, anyway), in the sense that is so dark and downbeat. But hands down my favorite D'Amato score—at least this year—is Carlo Maria Cordio's atmospheric, dreamy score for *Absurd*. It was one of his first scores in general, and also the beginning of a fruitful collaboration with D'Amato. (Fun fact: he also went on to score *Curse II: The Bite*, which is a trash film about radioactive mutant snakes that probably no one but me likes.) I love the *Absurd* score so much that it's set as both my alarm clock and ring tone.

Chief amongst D'Amato's collaborators in front of and behind the camera was Laura Gemser. Talk a bit about their collaborations and your thoughts.

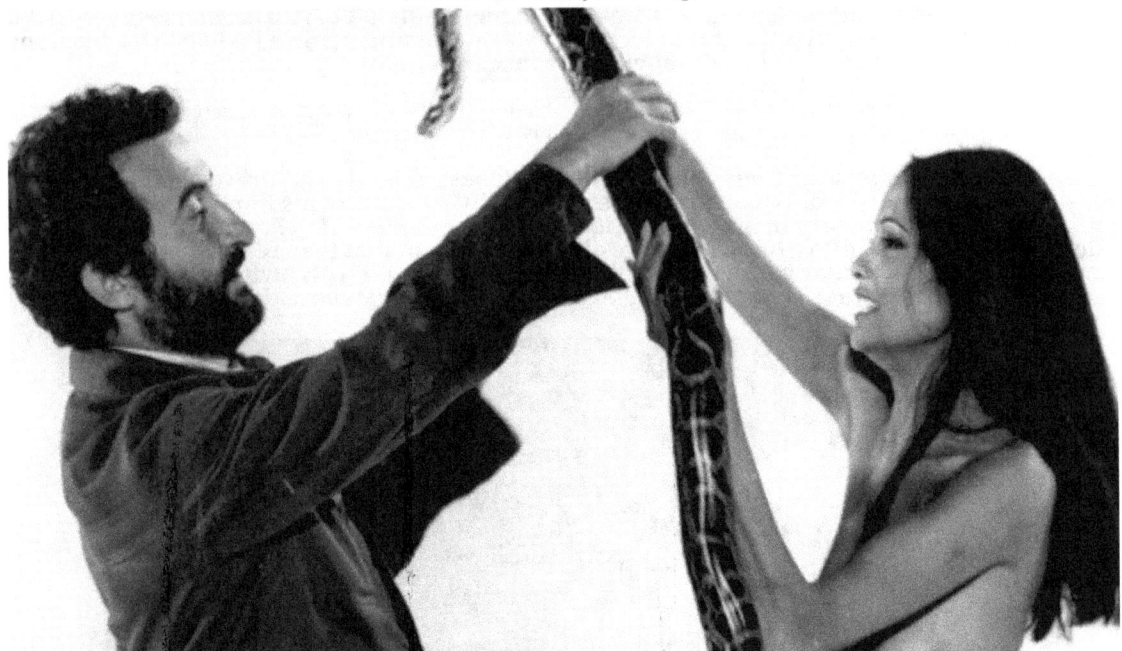

Dutch-Indonesian actress Laura Gemser has such a prominent role in D'Amato's cinema that you can't really consider it without her or as separate from her. She's in the majority of D'Amato's '70s films, though did occasionally work with other cult directors like Jose Larraz, Riccardo Freda, and Bruno Mattei. She appeared in primarily erotic dramas, though also adventure films and exploitation movies—including several not directed by D'Amato—and the first "Black Emanuelle" film was of course directed by Bitto Albertini, which is where Gemser originated the role. She also has a bit part in *Emmanuelle II* (1975), an interesting cross over between the series. Gemser became so iconic as Black Emanuelle (though she's Indonesian, not of African descent), that a number of other '70s films she was in were retitled so they appear to be part of the Emanuelle series. And for anyone who has no clue what I mean by Black Emanuelle, [Jeremy, feel free to cut this if you think it isn't helpful] it's a spin off series inspired by Just Jaeckin's *Emmanuelle* (1974), about the titular woman and the erotic adventures she gets into in exotic locales. That became a series in its own right, but enterprising exploitation directors like Albertini and D'Amato, made a spin off that cleverly dropped an 'm' and the original plot. "Emanuelle" is sometimes a photographer or journalist, but it's really just a stock role for Gemser. Outside of the Black Emanuelle films, she impressively continued working with D'Amato for well over two decades: she worked with him almost exclusively in the '80s, and even into the early '90s as her career died down. She is an absolute force of nature.

D'Amato seems to be having a much welcomed renaissance thanks to a number of recent special edition releases. Talk about these and which are the most important.

I'm terrible at selecting favorites, but I have to go ahead and say that teenage me is in a constant state of shock that we have D'Amato on blu-ray. I think the most important releases overall are the ones Severin are doing: *Beyond the Darkness, Emanuelle and the Last Cannibals, Absurd, Anthropophagus*, and soon to be *Emanuelle's Revenge* aka *Emanuelle and Francoise* (which is incredible and is not remotely a Black Emanuelle film, to further confuse anyone trying to get into the Emmanuelle/Emanuelle series). They come with great perks like toys, T-shirts, pins, and so on. On some level these add ons are silly, but that doesn't stop me from buying all of them and from feeling like it gives D'Amato the special treatment—and the respect—he's been lacking over the years.

For newbies what D'Amato film would you recommend as a good starting point?

I am a total failure when it comes to this question, partly because it depends on which genre you

are in the mood for. If you want really brutal, downbeat Eurohorror, *Beyond the Darkness*. For surreal gothic horror, go with *Death Smiles on a Murder*. Gore? *Absurd*. Exploitation? *Emanuelle and the Last Cannibals*. Fantasy-sword and sorcery-sci-fi? *Ator*. And so on. Part of what makes D'Amato so special is that he worked in nearly every genre and you have to be willing to let him take you on an adventure without having a lot of expectations ahead of time.

I've been more than a bit obsessed with *Buio Omega* since I first saw it back in the nineties and it remains my favorite D'Amato film. Is there a particular work in his filmography that reigns supreme in your view and why?

Why would you ask me this question? It's just mean. In all seriousness, if I had to answer I would probably also say *Buio Omega* because it's an old love. But I also have to say *Absurd*, because I'm morally obligated to name a title with George Eastman. I think both of these films show D'Amato on top of his form, for one thing. But for another, I'm a person who likes the strange and unusual. Both of these films are absolutely unlike anything else you'll see; watching either one is an experience, not just sitting down for a run of the mill horror movie. And I think that quality of unexpectedness, of originality, represents D'Amato at his best.

I think chief amongst his most underrated films is *Absurd*, which recently got a splendid special edition release. I really love that film and remain surprised that more fans don't seem to embrace it. What are your thoughts on it and is there a particular D'Amato film you would like to see get more recognition?

Absurd has really become one of my favorite D'Amato films thanks to Severin's recent blu-ray release. It was something that I saw as a teenager - on a crappy bootleg under a different title - but I only had hazy memories of it. For some reason I assumed it was some kind of alternate cut to *Anthropophagus* - which is probably reasonable considering they both contains loads of nonsensical gore and star George Eastman, and *Absurd* is often described as a sequel to *Anthropophagus* even though it isn't, really. *Absurd* has the same kind of unsettling, dreamlike quality that

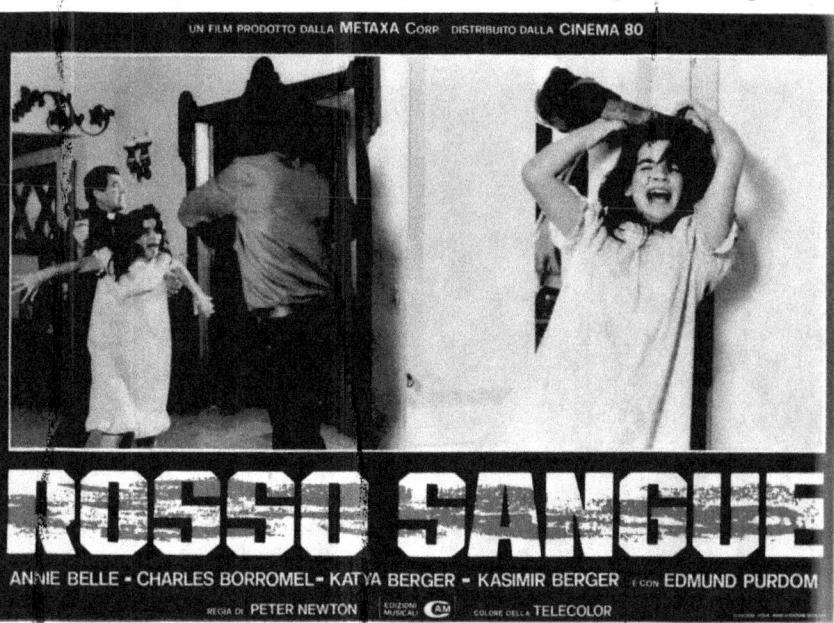

I think marks D'Amato's best films, and I don't think it would be out of line if you watched it as a triple feature with things like *Buio Omega* or *Death Smiles on a Murderer*. I almost don't want to address the plot - a priest tracks an inexplicably regenerating madman into a small town, where said madman (Eastman, of course), proceeds to wreak bloody havoc, ultimately winding up in the home of children whose parents have left them with a babysitter. But, as in many D'Amato films, the plot matters less than the eerie mood and the film really succeeds because of the way D'Amato plays with a number of genre tropes. He seems to consciously borrow from the budding slasher genre, while also making an effective film about our fears of the boogie man. In short, this is the film I wanted John Carpenter's *Halloween* to be, though I know that sentence is going to send at least one person into hysterics.

What are your thoughts on D'Amato's later adult work and how do you think it fits in with his filmography?

Honestly, one of my biggest pet peeves when people talk about hardcore films like they exist in some kind of ghetto. I am very tired of hearing genre fans say that directors like Franco, Rollin, and D'Amato made hardcore films in these hushed tones, like it's something we should be embarrassed about. I haven't seen all of these later films (there are like a hundred and some are hard to get ahold of), but overall if you like '90s porn—and I honestly don't know a lot of people who do—it's worth checking out. These are still D'Amato films, they just won't have the grain/texture of his '70s sex films, in terms of film quality, and they do lack some of the originality and some of the charm. Again, if you find yourself intrigued, there's no reason not to check a few out.

*** SAMM DEIGHAN CREATED THE INFLUENTIAL FILM BLOG SATANIC PANDEMONIUM AND SHE IS THE ASSOCIATE EDITOR OF DIABOLIQUE MAGAZINE AS WELL AS THE CO-HOST OF THE DAUGHTERS OF DARKNESS PODCAST. SHE EDITED THE ACCLAIMED BOOK LOST GIRLS: THE PHANTASMAGORICAL CINEMA OF JEAN ROLLIN FROM SPECTACULAR OPTICAL, AND HER BOOK ON FRITZ LANG'S M IS FORTHCOMING FROM AUTEUR PUBLISHING. SAMM CAN ALSO BE HEARD ON A NUMBER OF AUDIO COMMENTARIES ON VARIOUS BLU-RAY RELEASES WITH MORE COMING SOON. FOLLOW HER AT @ SAMMDEIGHAN, FACEBOOK.COM/SAMM.DEIGHAN AND INSTAGRAM.COM/SAMMDEIGHAN/***

AN INTERVIEW WITH

JUSTIN COFFEE

BY JEREMY R RICHEY

JR: Hey Justin, so great to feature you again!
(Justin was previously interviewed for *Art Decades*
and his portrait of Francoise Pascal featured on one of that publication's final volumes.)

When did you first become familiar with the films of Joe D'Amato?

JC: I first became aware of his work through films such as *Buio Omega* (*Beyond the Darkness*),
Death Smiles on a Murderer, *Anthropophagus* and *Absurd*.

JR: Was there a particular film of his that first really sparked your interest?

The one that most sparks my interest is probably *Beyond the Darkness* and *Death Smiles on a Murderer*. *Death Smiles on a Murderer* with its gothic giallo aesthetics really appeal to my love of that genre, plus it never hurts when you have Ewa Aulin as one of the leads.

His work is undergoing a bit of a renaissance thanks to a number of recent special edition releases, do you have a particular favorite?

At the moment probably *Death Smiles on a Murderer* is my favourite. I am looking forward to seeing *Emanuelle and Francoise* which is coming out from Severin, which is a remake of the 1968 Greek film directed by Dimi Dadiras, *The Wild Pussycat*. I highly recommend picking up that set from Mondo Macabro, which stars Gisela Dali who is quite a treat as a leading lady. Dali exudes the sensuality and danger that some of Jess Franco's leading ladies do.

When did you first see the shocking *Emanuelle in America* and what did you think of the film?

Surprisingly this was my first foray into *Emanuelle in America*. I was aware of the film, but had never gotten around to seeing it. It balances sensuality with the shocking elements well, though those parts are still rather scandalous even now.
Laura Gemser really carries the film with her presence, she is gorgeous. The character reminded me almost of Guido Crepax's Valentina, which was very appealing to me. T
he Nico Fidenco score is really ripe for a re-release on vinyl.

How did you become involved with the new special edition of the film?

After I finished up on the cover for Lucio Fulci's *Perversion Story*
it was presented as a possibility of another cover to work on, along with *The Wild Pussycat*.

Tell us a bit about your beautiful cover artwork for the release and what inspired it?

Usually I will watch the film, and take mental notes of scenes or certain shots that I feel sum up the film to me. Sometimes it just comes to you and other times it is a bit more work. It also comes down to a balance of looking at what has been done before as well and trying to offer something new. In this case I was paying homage to the UK quad poster for *Black Emanuelle*, a gorgeous piece of artwork done by Vic Fair. Mine pales in comparison to that, though I gave it my best shot.

What else are you currently working on and where is the best spot for fans to keep up with you and your work?

Currently I am working on various things, but due to NDA's and the such it makes it hard to specify. I am still creating new illustrations for marketing as well as working on some longterm projects. The best place for people to keep up with my work is Instagram (justin_coffee) probably, it's a bit dusty and needs to be updated, but hopefully soon I will post some new work! Thank you for the kind words and inquiring about my art.

FOLLOW JUSTIN'S INSTAGRAM FOR MORE OF HIS STRIKING WORK AND CHECK OUT MONDO MACABRO'S INCREDIBLE NEW BLU-RAY OF EMANUELLE IN AMERICA TO SEE HIS DAZZLING NEW ARTWORK IN ITS FULL COLOR GLORY!

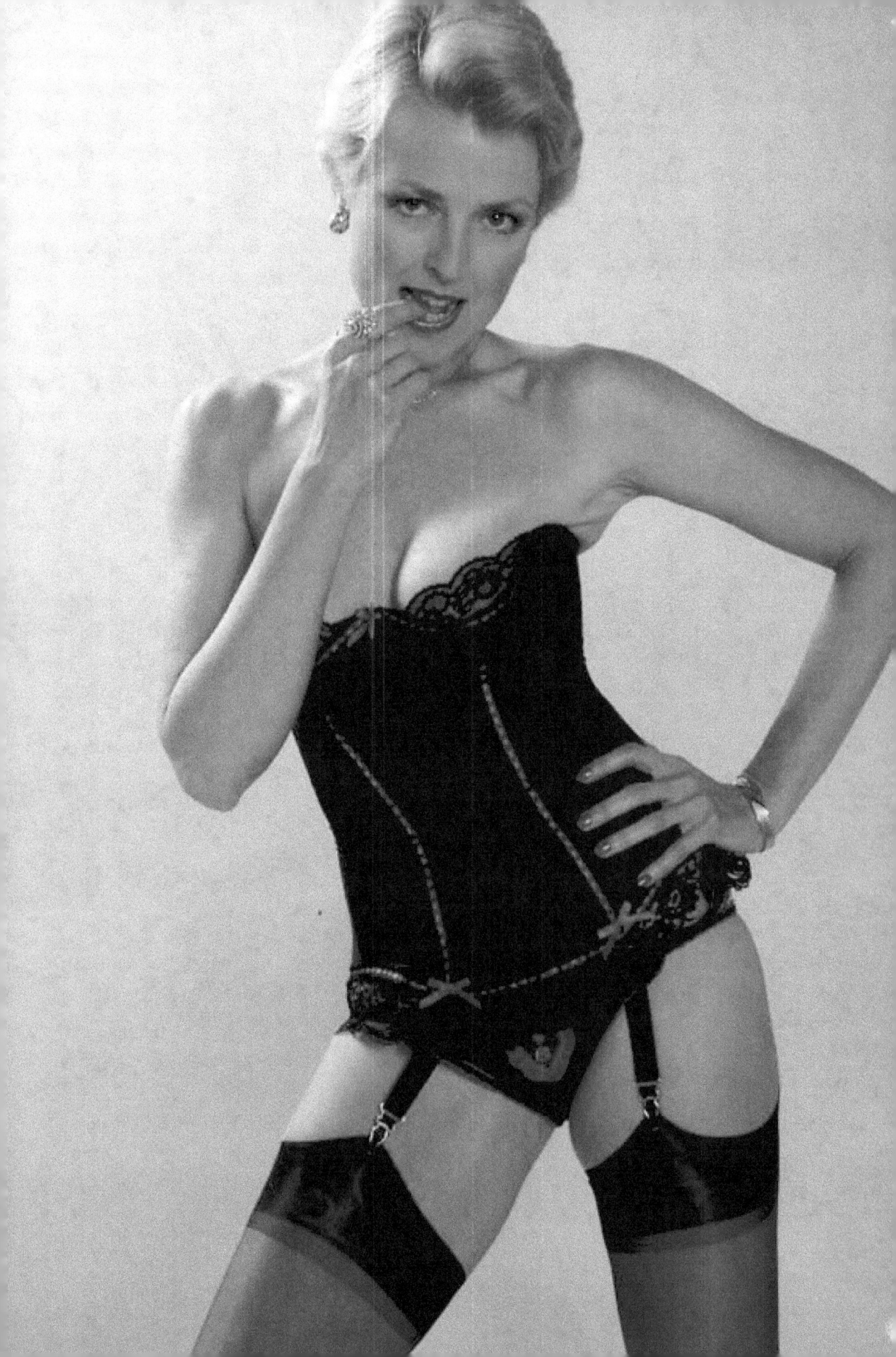

The Sensual World:
A Peek into Photographic Pioneer
Paul Johnson
by Heather Drain

Photographing the human body is a deceptively easy art form, especially if the figures are a mix of beautiful and handsome models in and out of various states of dress and each other. But anyone that has seen everything from the airbrushed-plastic-love-drones of latter-day *Playboy* to any number of older school grungy *Hustler*-Beaver-of-the-Month ripoffs, doing truly great photography involving the human body and especially lovemaking, is far from easy and when done badly, can be both greasy and worst of all, dull. But there is one pioneer of modern-day erotic photography whose work combined vibrant colors, pinpoint composition, and sheer skill without sacrificing any warm-fleshed-earthiness.

Ladies and gentlemen, let me introduce you to Paul Johnson. An incredibly nice, somewhat shy and humble man, Paul entered the world of nude and sex magazines as a photographer and occasionally model throughout the 1970s and '80s, getting his start in the Academy Press publication, the 1970 book, *Sex in Marriage*. From there, Paul forged a path that was completely his own, including his groundbreaking POV series, where his role as both model and photographer were one and the same. Keep in mind, POV (point-of-view) style in hardcore imagery is commonplace now in the digital age, but this was the 1970s. Even more impressive, is that Paul's talents as a photographer shined even when he was the lucky male on the receiving end of some amorous ladies' affection.

Whether he was in the shots or not, Paul Johnson's work is unified by three strong features: beautiful, near oil-pastel type colors, primed composition, and organic, warm sensuality. The sex in Paul's photography is natural, full of ease and genuine eroticism. There is nothing dirty about his work, except only in the best possible sweet and sensuous way. You can immediately look at a photo and tell whether or not Paul shot it, which is always the earmark of a good and true auteur. I was extremely lucky to interview Paul via email, with his answers further confirming that the man is as nice as he is honest and forthcoming.

What are some of the images and art (ie. film, music, books) that moved you as a kid before discovering erotica?

I always enjoyed pictures of all kinds and I could draw pretty well, won some honors in the local Spokane newspaper as young as 6 or 7. As I got a little older I started drawing nudes, mostly women and sometimes muscular men on my school notebooks when I was supposed to be paying attention to teachers. One thing that drew me to photography is the sharp reproduction which was better than I could draw or paint.

What was the spark that led you into photography?

The photos that moved me most were those 4 x 5 hard-core photo somebody gave me when I was 11 years old. When I first masturbated looking at them I imagined myself being that the guy in the picture and that's always been my fantasy is to be that guy in the picture, not the photographer. Then I found myself in the business of hiring men to live my fantasy and this was largely my motivation for doing POV. I don't believe I am the 1st to ever photographed someone giving them head but I was the 1st to have it published.

I didn't have a great interest in photography as a kid but I did have a simple camera, an Ansco Flash Clipper as I remember, that I enjoyed using. It was in my freshman year at Whitman College in Walla Walla, Wa. When I became interested in photography. I was majoring in fine art but all my photo work was out of school. It was with a buddy named Barney Blackman with whom I started playing with photography. We got a big push when we met a photographers widow who let us use her departed husband's well-equipped darkroom. I worked for 9 years as a surveyor for the Army Corp of Engineers building all those dams on the Snake River as my interest in photography grew. Barney had lost interest and moved on. During this time I developed Reynaud's syndrome which made me too susceptible to cold to continue working in the northwestern winters so I quit the Corps, drew out my retirement and, on a doctor's suggestion, moved south to Santa Barbara where I attend Brooks Institute of Photography.

On your website, you mention that you submitted some nude work to Elysium while you were still a college student at Brooks Institute of Photography. Did you have any foresight that this move would be your gateway into the more sensual and sexual photography?

When I made my first sale to Elysium I hoped that this would lead to more such sales as it was my fantasy to be a photographer of nudes and selling to various publications like my heroes Peter Gowland and Andre De Dienes but I had no idea that it would lead to hardcore porn, didn't even consider that as a possibility and never had the fantasy of shooting it. I did share the common fantasy of many photographers that maybe I might get laid in the process of photographing a nude, didn't really happen all that often, partly because I am quite shy and not likely to make a move unless a pretty broad opening was made.

Your photography, including both your "Art of Paul Johnson" series and the erotica, have such a standout vibrancy and warmth that set them apart from any other photographer out there. Part of that is your obvious skill with working with models. What is part of your key approach with working with talent?

As to your question about my ability to work with people — that harks back to the 1st unit at Brooks when at the final critique when Mr. Bogie singled me out by being the only student to who he suggested a path forward when he said to me "you have an ability to get people to do things in front of a camera so you should work with people," I think that ability is innate and has always been there although I think respect for my subjects has a lot to do with it and I'm un-threatening. A lot of shoots they are so general I can work almost anyone in them. I didn't try to fit people into slots that didn't fit. On interviews, I always asked about their own personal fantasies or lifestyle and if they fit something or suggested something that's how I would work with them [I didn't count the 3-way fantasy, it's too common]. A good example of the proper fit was when I met Kaye Buckley and found that she had an alternate persona as Kazaba, a pleasure slave which of course I had to shoot. Kaye did the final edit on it using her own words, we're still good friends.

Also, I didn't hold myself above my models in any way as some of my competitors did. That also figures with me doing POV and being the only pornographer to put his body on the line in the magazines as the models do. For many years I avoided showing my face because LA. Vice knew me too well but eventually I did by allowing *Gourmet* to publish photos showing my face. It never caused any problem. When I was doing POV I assumed it was illegal but only in the aspect that I was paying for sex like a john, so what if I get busted as a john, I'm a pornographer already and it would be no big deal. Years later I had a lawyer check that out and I could have been busted for pandering, much more serious than being a john. Thankfully I never had problems with it and now the Statute of Limitations has run out.

Another thing about POV, one fantasy I had was that a connection would go past the brief sexual play of the shoot and sometimes it did. I played with a few off camera which was fine but the real joy are those where we connected deeper. Juliet Anderson was one as was Christine Kelly, my assistant before Juliet and who helped me on the shoot with Juliet and Holly McCall. Also, Carol Tong and I became close after a POV. Kaye Buckley is also an alumni of POV but our 1st sexual encounter is mentioned on that Pleasure Slave link. Bonnie Holiday sorta fits in there. Although we never had sex off camera we became friends and years later hired me to do photography for her. I'm still in touch with these women except for Juliet, we had breakfast about 2 weeks before she died. She told me several times "we'll always be friends" and she was right.

You got to work with some of the most beautiful and striking actresses and actors of the Classic era of Adult film, with names like Juliet Anderson, Nina Hartley, Mai Lin, Annette Haven, Jamie Gillis, Richard Pacheco, Sue Nero, Serena, Tawny Pearl, and so many more. With that, did you ever consider going into film after finding such big success in the magazine field?

With a partner, I did a movie at Brooks that won best of class award but I've never seriously considered movie work, my 1st love was still photography and I wanted to stay with that. If I had stayed in the biz —I left in '85 largely because of the AIDS scare, didn't want anyone, including me, catching it on my watch and using condoms was not an option for me. To me when condoms are used it is no longer porn but sex education— I would probably have done videos mostly because of how easy they are for POV, so much easier than a Hasselblad with a 40mm lens and film that has to be changed.

Are there any erotica photographers that you're a fan of? (Ala Just Jaeckin, Helmut Newton, Guy Bourdin, Chris von Wangenheim, etc.)

I haven't kept up with the photography field and the only erotic photographer you mentioned that I am aware of is Helmut Newton who has done some cool stuff but I wouldn't call myself a fan in that I don't follow him but enjoy his work when I see it.

You were the first still photographer that got to work with industry legend and femme-phenom, Nina Hartley. What was it like working with Nina in those early years of her career?

Working with Nina Hartley early in her career was a lot like my experience with Juliet Anderson or any other richly talented model where I was aware that this person is likely to become a star. It's not that much different from working with anyone new except for this awareness. Having people like these in front of my camera makes my life easy and more fun. I gave very little direction. sorta turning them loose and it becomes more of a 3-way, or more, dance with me being very involved psychically and physically always moving with my camera. The other side of that is if I have models who are just that, models I have to mold, I could direct every move, the models would have fun because I direct fun porn sex, it would take less time and it would usually end up looking fine. A clarification: When a person is doing a mag layout they are a model, but in a film they're an actor.

Some of your best work was with the absolutely stunning and charismatic Juliet Anderson. While most viewers may know her more as "Aunt Peg," what were some of her traits that may surprise them?

Now about Juliet. One of her traits that made her a good assistant was that she could be real bossy which helped keep things on track during shoots as that is a trait where I am weaker. An inside joke between us is that although she mastered my Hasselblad 500Cs which are quite complicated she couldn't master flicking a Bic, usually took a few tries, so this was a running joke between us as we smoked quite a bit of pot together and with friends. Juliet, being my assistant was part of my life, she hung out at the commune I lived in, she was friends with my kids, lover/partner, and many friends so she was a big part of my social life even joining in 3-ways with lovers. Juliet, my close friend, my ex-lover Emily, and Caitlyn who was my current lover at the time set up a house on Richmond Blvd. In Oakland where they turned tricks, sometimes called themselves "Paul's girls" although I had no part in their business. I often was there waiting for an appointment to end. I was also there for some interesting parties including Christmas and my birthday.

Juliet could be extremely shy when she wasn't being Juliet Anderson, porn star but just plain Judy Carr. I was there one time when she arrived, through the back door, late at a party at the Richmond House and had a bit of a panic attack. Caitlyn and I hung out with her in the kitchen till she was settled. Juliet was easier to be with when she was out of her porn star persona, that is the Juliet I drove up the coast with, in my van, the one with the King sized bed in the back.

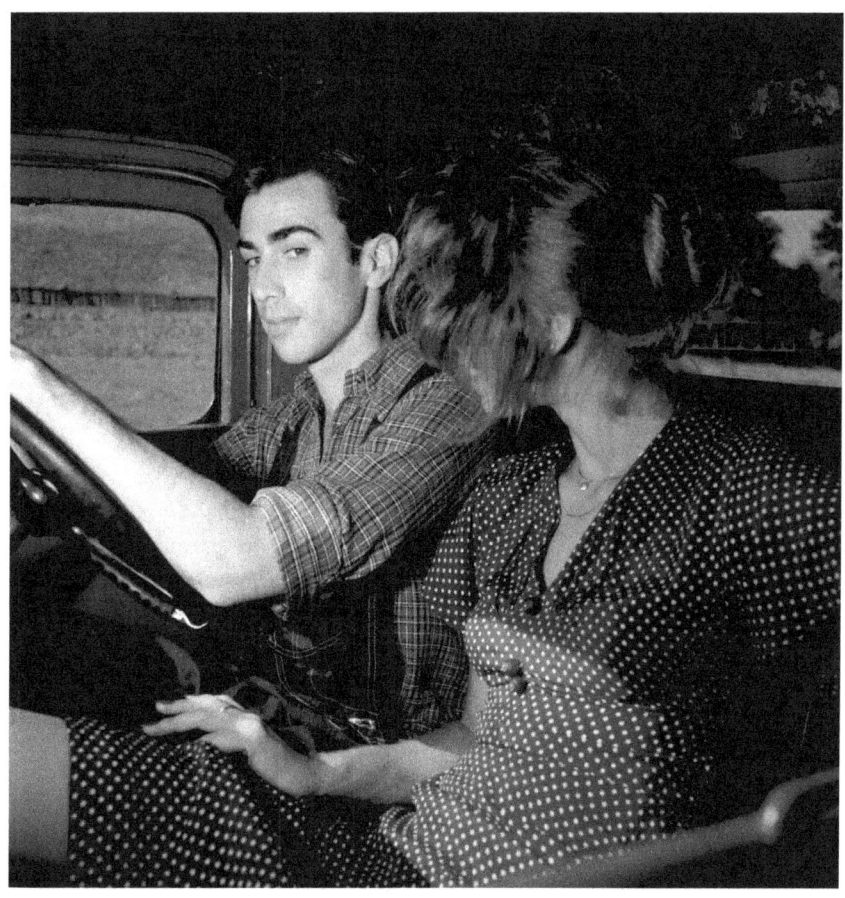

What advice would you give to any burgeoning artist?

The only advice I have for anyone starting out is to do what turns you on, pretty much what I did. Also, and this came from my EST seminar— There is a lot of funny biz in the biz, a lot of ripping off, padding accounts, and I played the game too. An early lesson was when I started at *Jaybird* a couple long time staff photographers showed me how to pad our very generous expense accounts. The only rule that was off limits was don't cheat the models. So what EST did was turn me around to where I played it straight with everyone. The 1st thing I did was go to a publisher who had been ripping me off, confronted him by telling him I was no longer going to do business with him because he has been ripping me off. It was shortly after that that things really started going my way. The Connoisseur Series was born and new things unfolded. It was almost abrupt how fast things turned around. So the advice is play it straight & honest although I know nothing of what the biz is like now.

Are there any current adult photographers, filmmakers and/or actors that you're a fan of?

As to current filmmakers and/or actors: I am not current with modern porn, I don't follow it so don't know much about who's around now. Even when I was active I lived in my own little niche and didn't see very many porn movies except for a few Grand Openings where I knew the people that made them or were in them, mostly Howard Ziehm & Bill Osco productions from the earliest days in LA. One of the things going on was my personal life away from porn was more interesting and erotic than what could be seen in a movie. Some models, Juliet for one, blended over into my private life but mostly it was populated by women who had nothing to do with porn. I've had a few sexual experiences that would be near impossible to film.

Although you might say I was the fan of many of the stars I knew it was as a fan of who they are, not the roles they played. As close to Juliet as I was I've never seen a whole movie that she was in, only a few sex scenes. When I masturbate I don't want to watch people I know but prefer the total anonymousness of complete strangers, still do. Currently, when I look at porn it's the free stuff online and what strikes me is how shoddy it is compared to the Golden Age. I don't have any moral problem with using the free stuff, I've been taken by the biz enough I figure it owes me.

Rudy Ray Moore biographer and guru of classic adult era ephemera Mark Murray may have said it best about Paul Johnson, when he wrote the following: "It's a shame that Paul's work has not yet been largely celebrated mostly due to his credit being absent in the magazines he produced. Yet, there is a distinctive style and authenticity to his work that was rarely seen then or now. He proudly calls himself as *pornographer* but I also see him as a sex enthusiast, talented artist, and one hell of a lucky man to be able to combine those loves together for a truly amazing career. He carved out a niche for himself that I don't think anyone else from that period did. He is definitely an innovator in several ways and should be recognized today. Paul spent his life doing what he was born to do and to this day he maintains his enthusiasm about sex and his life's work." Beautifully put and may we all soon see an era where an artist like Paul can get the proper respect and evaluation that he richly has earned.

To see and purchase some of Paul's art, including copies of his magazine work, you can visit his website at paulsfantasy.com.

Photos courtesy of Paul Johnson.

RAISED WITH A FILM BOOK IN HER HANDS, HEATHER DRAIN HAS BEEN CAPTIVATED BY THE LANGUAGE OF CINEMA SINCE DAY ONE. BORN AND RAISED IN ARKANSAS, SHE WENT FROM WRITING LEONARD MALTIN STYLED REVIEWS OF TITLES RANGING FROM **CEMETERY HIGH** TO **WOMEN ON THE VERGE OF A NERVOUS BREAKDOWN** IN THE FIFTH GRADE TO WRITING FOR PUBLICATIONS LIKE **VIDEO WATCHDOG,** **THE EXPLOITATION JOURNAL, LUNCHMEAT, ART DECADES, CASHIERS DU CINEMART, SCREEM** AND **THE LITTLE ROCK FREE PRESS** SEVERAL YEARS LATER. SHE HAS ALSO BEEN A CONTRIBUTOR TO **DANGEROUS MINDS, DIABOLIQUE, THE RIALTO REPORT, PARACINEMA, CINEMA HEAD CHEESE, CULTCUTS** AND, ON OCCASION, AS A GUEST WRITER, OVER AT BOTH **RUPERT PUPKIN SPEAKS** AND TURNER CLASSIC'S **MOVIE MORLOCKS** BLOG.

SHE LIVES WITH HER PAINTER/WRITER HUSBAND, C.F. ROBERTS AND THEIR TWO WONDERFUL AND SEMI-SURLY RESCUE CATS, ZIGGY AND TALLULAH. **FROM MONDOHEATHER.COM**

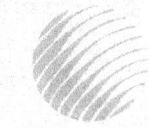

NEW WORLD PICTURES

PROUDLY PRESENTS

A SPECIAL
EVENING
WITH
VERONICA HART
and
CHUCK
VINCENT

Presenting
Their New Film

CLEO/ LEO

at
FILM FORUM

OCT. 17th 1989

Tickets are 5.50
with
a Q&A
and Reception
following the film.

The theater is located at
209 West Houston Street,
New York, NY 10014,
between 6th Avenue and
Varick (7th Avenue).

There is parking in the area
on most of the surrounding
streets, both metered &
non-metered.

Parking on 6th Avenue,
7th Avenue, & Varick is
metered.

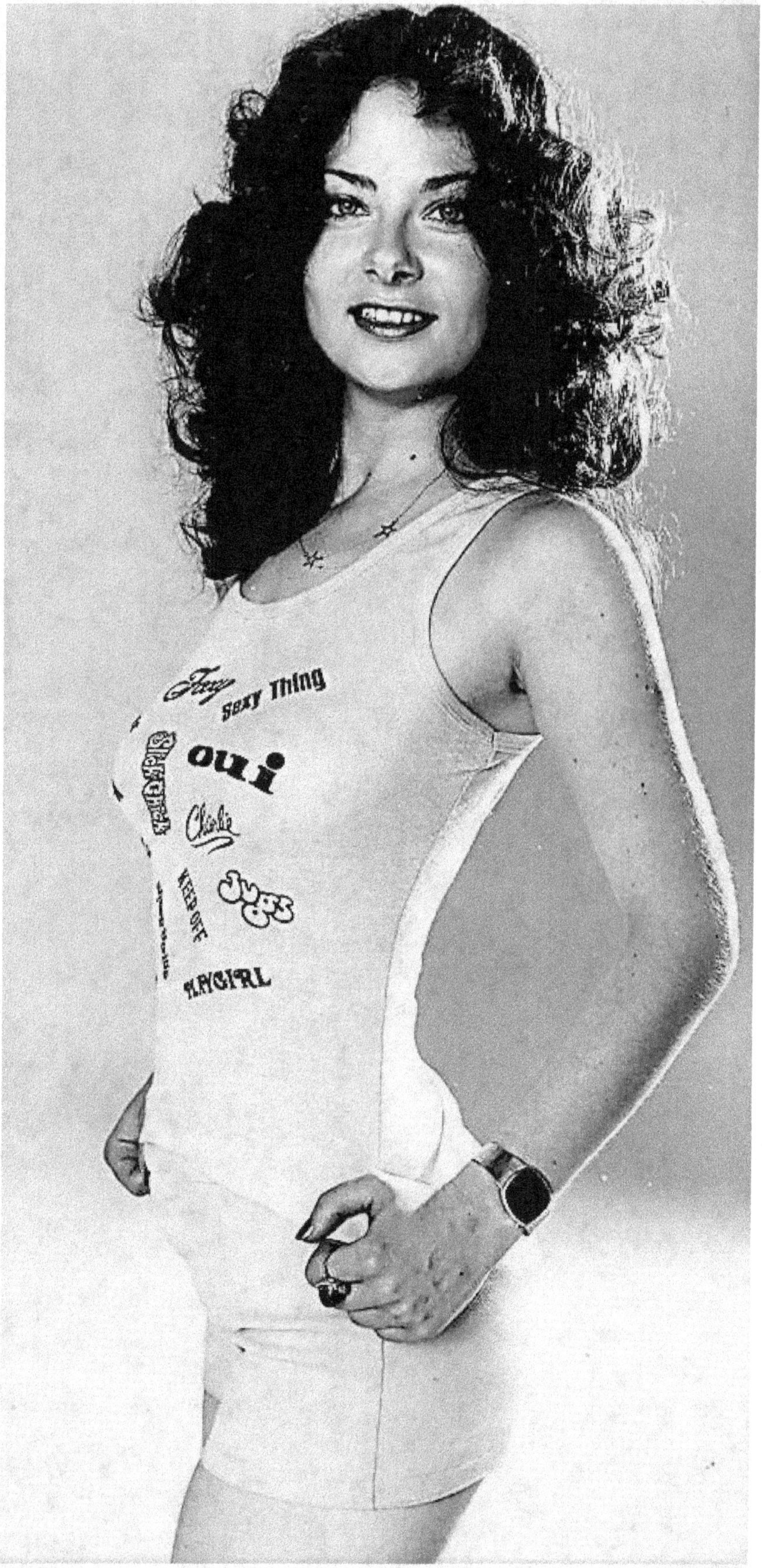

FEATHER BED

Les Bohem

*"If I had listened to what my mama said I'd be sleeping in a feather bed
All my sins been taken away."*

Hand My Down my Walking Cane - Traditional

Los Angeles, California - 1969

"If you've got to mumble, I wish you'd mumble to yourself," Reina said to Elvira. She didn't mean to sound so nasty; she was just tired. They were sitting together in the television lounge of Birnkrant. Reina was trying to read the textbook on women's culture that had been assigned in her women's literature class. Elvira was watching TV. Elvira pronounced her name with the "i" long as in "virus." She was Reina's roommate.

The hospital-tan walls of the television room flickered in the corners of Reina's vision around the pages of the book she stared at. On the TV, a housewife was recommending Tide for your wash. Reina had just read that grade school children, when asked whether daddies were smarter than mommies, had nearly all said yes, daddies were.

"I was just going to tell you about his roommate?" Elvira pouted. She was twenty, she wore her hair in a flip, and she was studying for her teaching credential.

Reina threw her book down next to a McCall's magazine on the metal-legged table with the thick glass top that sat in front of her. She closed her eyes.

She was standing in the Arctic, with blinding white all around her. The howl of an Arctic fox filled the cold air, coming softly at first and then rising into her ears. Often she found herself gliding into this freezing realm. She would feel cold, feel alone, and quickly shake herself back into the warm California dormitory. Tonight, she played it out. The howl of the fox relaxed her and even warmed her without fear; the bright white glowed soothing around her.

Elvira saw Reina put the book down and thought that she had put it down to listen. She continued her story, speaking every sentence as if it were a question, and raising her eyebrows more out of habit than to see if Reina had heard her. She no longer bothered Reina; Reina was not listening.

"Well you remember that gawky Oriental guy, Stanley, that was in our English class last semester? His father's a policeman, you know? He started sitting with me and Cathy at dinner every night? He was awful? He eats like a pig and he's got really terrible skin? He kept asking me out? So finally, I ran out of excuses and I didn't want to hurt his feelings so I said, 'Yes'?" Her eyebrows went higher than usual and she paused for a moment to catch her breath.

A black dot was appearing far out over the white; the fox had stopped howling but the wind had come up loud instead. Reina felt the snow between her toes. It felt warm and good.

"He came over last night to pick me up and he was five minutes early too? When we were halfway across the parking lot, he remembered he'd forgotten the tickets, so we walked all the way across the campus to Stonier and went up to his room to get them? It's the room with the tie-dyed curtains on the end next to the fire escape? I walked in and who do you think was sitting on the top bunk? In his underwear? That beautiful guy with the long hair that always eats by himself? I could hardly speak? He had such a gorgeous body? Stanley introduced us? It was his roommate? His name was Andrew? What a wonderful sounding name? He's so cute, I was really embarrassed of him seeing me with Stanley?"

The spot grew bigger as it approached. Some kind of an animal, stalking towards her. She had never stayed this long before. She wanted to call to the animal but the words wouldn't come and she watched silently as it approached.

"The rest of the night was just terrible? We went to the Shrine to see some awful band? Stanley kept screaming in my ear how great Janis Joplin had been? I could hardly hear him anyway so I just nodded my head and smiled? He said Andrew was a real good musician and played the Conga drums? We sat down on the floor and he started kissing me, 'cause it's so dark in there? He was really sloppy and he slobbered all over my chin? I didn't know what to do 'cause I mean after all he did buy the tickets and so I just let him kiss me, you know? I didn't know what he'd tell Andrew? It's real hard to see in there 'cause of all those weird lights, and he got like all gropy? But he didn't have any class, you know? Then finally I told him we had eleven o'clock lockout and got him to leave? When we were outside, I told him I was late and ran across the parking lot and he kind of ran after me? I went in right away before he even got there? Today, he was sitting with Andrew at lunch, so I really wanted to go up and sit with them, but I didn't know what to do?"

The spot was close now. She had followed its paw prints in the snow until it was near and she could see that it was a huge, proud lion, and she looked into its eyes. They were warm, twinkling with cat laughter. The lion threw its head back and roared, then looked back at her, its eyes still shining with savage laughter. She screamed high and long, her voice echoing off the snow, and when she stopped, the wall was hospital-tan in front of her.

"Well I know it wasn't a nice thing to do, but I didn't want to hurt his feelings?" Elvira said with another pout.

Reina was a child of the late sixties, just too young to ride the crest of the wave, maturing in the cynical swamp of Manson and poison acid that followed the first cloud-burst of peace, love, and flowers. She felt that she had somehow missed something; that she had no generation.

She had grown up in Encino, in the San Fernando Valley of Los Angeles. She lived with her father, her brother and her stepmother in an expensive tract off of Sepulveda. They had moved to the house when she was three years old, two months after her mother died. She didn't remember her mother at all.

She remembered the nurse who had moved in with them to take care of her little brother. Her name was Miss McCann. She was fat and oily and she smoked Benson and Hedges cigarettes. She would crush you in her lap against her big breasts and tell you stories about knights rescuing maidens. These were the only stories she seemed to know and all that ever changed were the names of the knight and the lady and the dangers that she was rescued from. The knights were always tall and strong and their lances glinted in the heroic sunlight as they rode off to do battle. The first day they came to the new house, Reina stepped on a rusty nail while exploring the back yard. Miss McCann spent the afternoon, while they waited for the doctor, telling about her uncle who had died of lockjaw because they couldn't figure out how to feed him. It was the only time Reina remembered her telling about anything but knights and ladies. She laughed and the fat shook under her chin.

When her brother, Michael, was older, their father would take them on long rides across Decker Canyon to the beach. The first time that Michael saw the ocean, he ran right up to it and took a big drink. She could still see the look of shock on his face. It was as if the world had just lied to him.

Their father was a psychologist. He brought Michael a rat on his fifth birth-day. He remarried when Reina was ten. She had seen it coming in the lines of sadness slowly lifting from under his eyes. When he looked at her now, he wasn't always saying. 'You look just like your mother' somewhere inside.

Regan was funny and pretty and Michael and Reina liked her right away.

She came on rides to the beach with them. She packed wonderful picnic lunches. She taught them both how to play the guitar.

By the time Reina was in high school, Regan was her closest friend. These were the years of protest. Reina wrote angry poems for the school paper and organized a boycott to protest dress code regulations. She went on anti-war marches and wore a black armband to school. She wrote romantic stories in her notebooks and only showed them to Regan. She would bring her friends to her house where they would sit on the Danish Modern furniture, drinking coffee with her father and Regan out of brightly enameled coffee cups, and talking about the Berkeley demonstrations, the Huelga grape boycott, whether or not the Beatles would really break up.

The summer before she left for college was the first real high school summer Reina had had. Warm evenings looking at the lights of the valley with her friends; parties and intrigues. She had hated Birmingham High School for three years, and now she found herself wishing more and more that she didn't have to leave.

One night in August, a month before her seventeenth birthday and two weeks before she was to leave for school, Reina went to a party at Zuma beach. Her friends had come over and she'd borrowed her father's Pontiac. A girl named Mimi, whom Reina had only met once before, came with them. She brought a gram of hash. They passed the pipe as she drove them over Decker Canyon, going the way her father had always taken when they were little.

She parked the car in an almost empty lot and stepped out into the warm beach breeze. Her friends quickly vanished off towards a bonfire on the beach, whooping and yelling greetings. Around the bonfire she could see familiar faces, kids from school whose names she didn't know or couldn't remember. She didn't feel now like going to a party.

She walked away from the fire, moving around a cliff, so that the party noises were cut by the sound of the sea. She sat, watching the ocean.

After a while, she started to sing a song that Regan had once taught her, her voice echoing quiet off the water. *"When I wore my apron low, couldn't keep you from my door. All my sins been taken away, taken away."*

There was a howl behind her. A comical sound, someone pretending to be a dog baying at the moon. She stopped singing and turned around. A boy with curly blond hair stood grinning behind her. He was wearing jeans and a dirty white t-shirt with the sleeves rolled up to his shoulders. He had a pack of cigarettes stuck in one of

...he rolled up shirt sle...s. He held a can of beer and a cigarette in one hand; the other rested on his hip. She had seen him at the fire, just before she'd walked away to sit by the sea.

"That was real pretty singing," he grinned, throwing his head back and howling again. He moved to sit next to her, flicking his cigarette onto the wet sand where it hissed and went out. "Real pretty. What're you trying to do, scare the fishes?" He laughed mechanically, his head swinging up and down as if it were on hinges.

"That's a real major party they got going on down there, you know?" He nodded his head back over the cliff. "Phil Augustine and Radkie just threw that chick Susie, with the blond hair, into the water. She's soaked so bad you can see right through her blouse." He head stopped swinging and he looked at her with a leer.

She smiled back automatically, looking at the moonlight twinkling off the sea. It was like an animated science film she'd once seen about chromosomes.

"Ya want some beer or a cigarette?" He offered the can.

"No thanks, I don't really feel like it."

He took a last pull and threw the can away, then lit another cigarette.

"What're you doing sitting here by yourself, huh?"

"I just didn't feel like being around a lot of people right now." She didn't look at him. He moved a little closer, waving his cigarette in the air as he spoke.

"I seen you when you guys all came. I was hoping I'd get a chance to talk to you. I been seeing you around school. You're fine, real fine."

He waited for her to answer. She didn't. He went on. "My name's Louie. I used to live around here when I was a kid, you know, but my folks moved the San Diego and we only came back last year. I just started at Birmingham last semester."

"Did you go to grammar school here?" she asked for something to say.

"Just 'til second grade. I had some teacher named Lumquat or something at Cowell Street."

"Really, Miss Loquist? So did I."

"No shit. You mean we're old friends?"

She tried smiling again. "What's your last name?" she asked.

"Haskell."

"I remember you. Did you always sit in the back row next to the heater?"

"Yeah, that was me."

"You had freckles?"

"Still do."

"You were always rattling the heater with your pencil."

They sat quietly for some moments.

She watched the ocean again. The lights danced. He started to say something once, then stopped. Then he pulled her clumsily towards him and kissed her on the mouth. She struggled back up asking, "What are you doing?" in a voice that sounded high and strange to her. Someone else's voice.

"Just trying to be friendly. It's a party for Christsakes, What'd you come for anyway?"' His head bobbed up and down on its hinges, like a grinning jack-in-the-box.

"Please go away," she said.

"Aw come on. You know why you walked down here. You can't tell me."

"Go away, please," she repeated.

"Come on. You know, free love."

"Away."

"We could have some fun."

"Leave me alone."

"Give me a taste for old Miss Loquim," He pushed her back on the sand. Her eyes rose past the moon to the night sky above. There was one greenish star shining through the moonlight. "You can't tell me," Louie repeated, panting, "I know what you want." He began fumbling with her pants with one hand, pushing the other up under her blouse, grabbing her breasts. His hands felt sandy and cold. She stared at the green star, so cool and far away. She didn't move at all.

He forced her pants and panties down around her knees and began probing her with his finger while his other hand still pawed at her breasts, pinching the nipples hard. He stopped for a moment to undo his fly.

"Let's work that little noodle," he said, his finger around as if he were trying to smudge out a mistake on a blackboard.

She lay perfectly still, hardly aware that the finger hurt her. It was further away than the green star. He rubbed harder. "Got to get that love juice flowing," he said. He moved his hands below her and climbed on top of her. She stared at his face. It was sweaty and ugly. His eyes were closed, his nostrils flared slightly. His mouth had locked in a crooked grin. A thin trail of drool dripped from its side. His freckles had faded. He pulled her up over him. He was covered with sand, coarse and scraping. Still she lay without moving, never looking away from his straining face with the moon directly behind it, making it glow like a fungus.

"A goddamned cherry." He grunted, dug harder. She knew it hurt terribly. She thought of the ways it hurt, like sand paper, and the deeper ache. But it was all far away. She looked straight into his ugly, popping face as he pushed and scraped harder and harder and deeper until everything popped at once and he jumped off her, tearing himself back out and wiping the sand and blood off on his underwear before zipping his pants back up.

She watched the moon, feeling nothing. He bent to pick up the pack of cigarettes that had fallen from his shirtsleeve. There were big patches of sweat under his arms.

"If you get me in any trouble, you little bitch, I'll get Wade and Radkie and we'll give it to you right." He smiled at her, picked a tooth with a fingernail, and stood up. "Remember the four 'f's, baby. Find 'em, feel em, fuck em, forget 'em." He laughed and disappeared around the cliff to join the party.

She watched the moon and the green star for a while without thinking, and then she stood up and pulled on her pants. There was a little blood in the sand. She kicked at it with her toe until it disappeared. She was very cold and she went up the cliff to the car to wait for her friends.

No one talked in the car on the way home. Reina drove and the others stared uncomfortably out the windows into the darkness with the sense that something irrevocable had happened. There was no one in the car that Reina wanted to talk to, no one to whom she could tell what had happened. She knew that she had no friends and she began to cry quietly as she drove for being so alone.

She left the television room and went back upstairs. Elvira had the lower bunk; Reina had asked her for the upper. She climbed into her bed and lay, waiting. The dormitory noises faded and she was in the Arctic again. It was blinding white. The fox howled, softly. She waited. Now the lion came. This time she couldn't scream and she let it come on. Its eyes laughed. It came right up to her and stared at her and licked her face gently, like a puppy.

Les Bohem is a musician, poet and screenwriter from Los Angeles. As a musican, he was a member of Sparks and Gleaming Spires He released his acclaimed solo album
Moved to Duarte in 2016.
As a screenwriter he has written
A Nightmare on Elm Street 5: The Dream Child, *Daylight* and *Dante's Peak* among a number of others.
Find out more about him at lesbohemswonderfulworldoflesbohem.com/ and order his new books
Old Friends at A Party and *Junk* at

prolificpress.com/bookstore/
and
audible.com/pd/Junk-Audiobook/
B07D1B9SD5.

COMING SOON TO A NIGHTMARE NEAR YOU

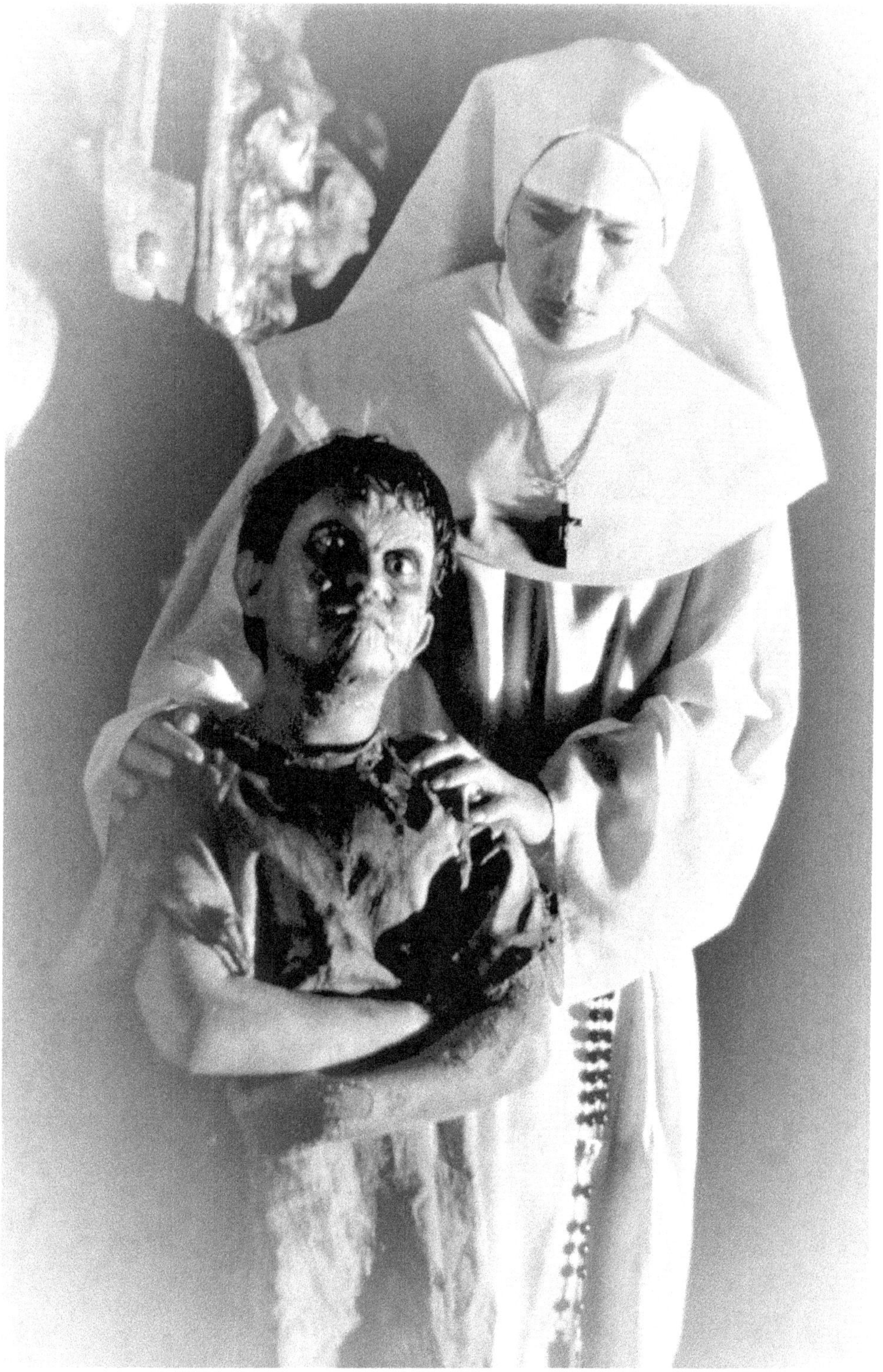

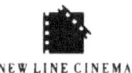

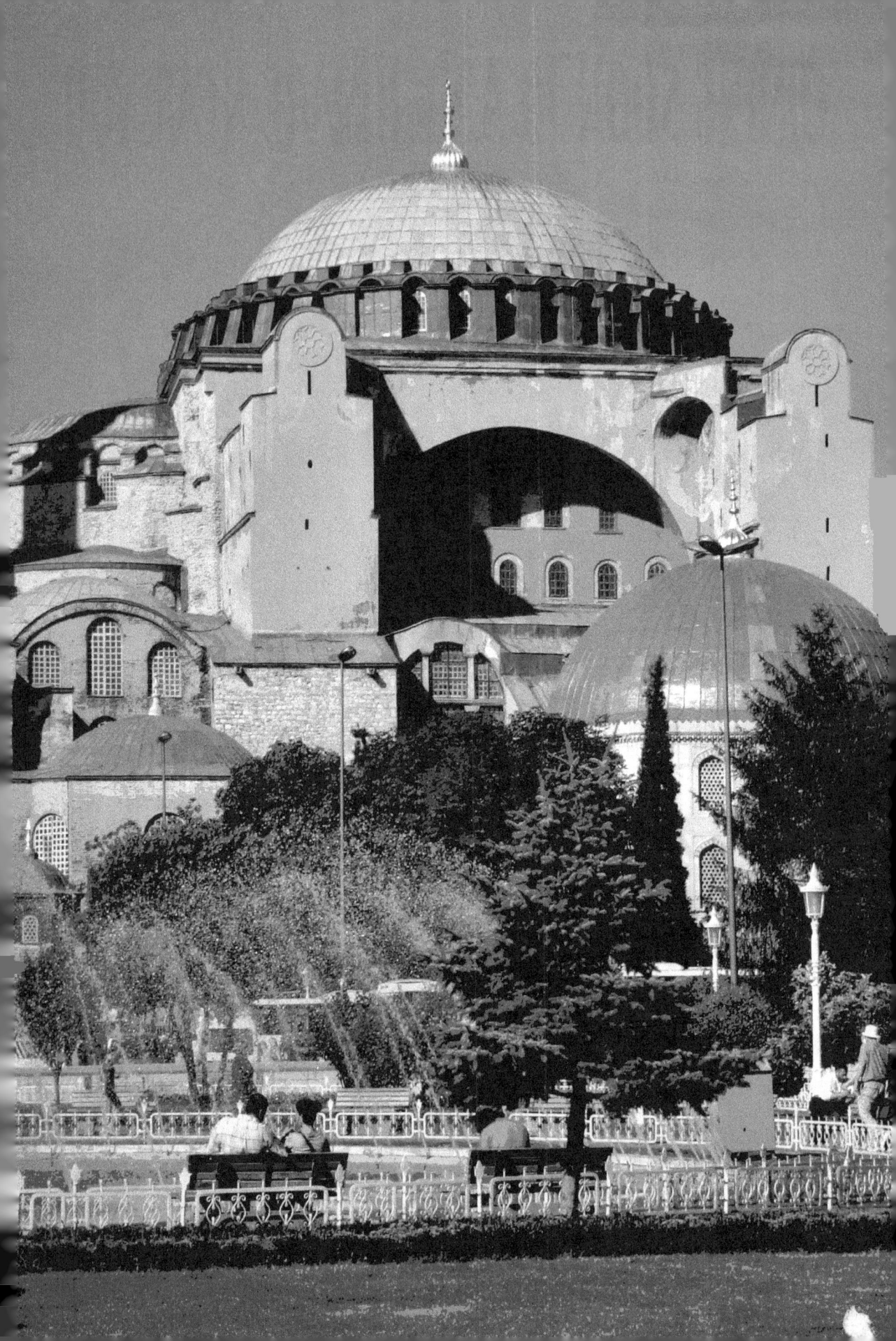

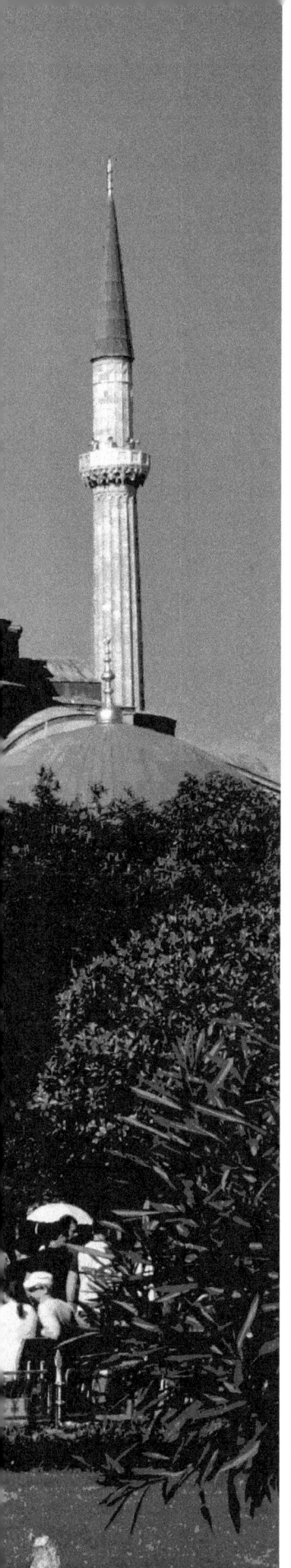

THE INSTANBUL GNOSIS

By

Robert Monell

Communion with the dead is always a dangerous business.
I found that out the hard way. It was a psy-op created by
powers that had me targeted. A burning mist had settled
over Istanbul, much the same way it had become a permanent shroud for Beijing and other Eastern cities. My role
was Tracer, Agent of Zedd. I had received my instructions
through psi transference shortly before the 12 AM, New
Year. I had been in a cloud alley and a black cat crossed
my path. Not being superstitious I turned my attention to
my target, an out of control female Synthetic which had
two heads, one normal, one rather like a turtle. She emerged
from the emerald mist slowly and I sent a capsule right at
her, which resulted in melting her completely in very short
order.

Stasis was my operational status at that time. I wasn't free
for any real or illusory travel. That would change. The
next morning I checked into the Upstate New York Clinic,
where my presence had been prearranged by a designated
team of consultants. It was winter and the clinic was sit-
uated nine levels beneath a frozen graveyard in a rural
area. I had no idea about how important the concepts of
"layers" was in living life with one's eyes open. So that's
why I'm making this memoir, speaking into a file which
will be saved, edited and transmitted to a cloud-capsule.
I have to concentrate on the search. My own destruction
aside, I need to find and understand what Simone left for
me before she disappeared. Her professor said there was
a thought file floating around the agitation chamber. I
would take the medication later, when I had assimilated the
report. She had tremendous psi powers, but I depended upon
the soft machinery in my brain. The scene was encased in
a theoretical capsule which replaced in what used to be
called cyberspace. Now, it was hyper reality in Ultra-Plasma High-Density Cold-Dark-Matter capsules [UPHDCDMcaps]. I
accessed several before I began the investigation. It could
also be a free-floating cloud or sonic iterations. Nothing
was lost anymore. Not like it used to be when something was
stored in human memory, or in a notebook, or on a recording,
a film, a video, some kind of disc or drive, all unreliable
platforms.

Ultra level #1 had a protagonist, a 15th Century entity which arrived on a meteor which fell on the dark side of the Earth's moon. Several obscure astronomers knew of the incident but feared to make it known to the scientific or civil authorities of the day. Simone said she knew of a woman in Constantinople who knew of the fall and its aftermath. I knew she was right because I was there when the city fell. I experienced all of it not through my own eyes but as if in a film in which I was a character. The entity was the camera which both shot and projected the film. Perhaps film is the wrong word because film as a physical thing hadn't existed for a long time. There had been video, digital, virtual reality, holograms, and much more. The Ultra-Plasma was now a universal medium. No devices of any kind were necessary. No projectors, screens, receivers, amplifiers or enhancers.

If it were a film playing in a 20th century mall Ultra level # 1 would open with an overhead view of several cannons being dragged into place at strategic locations around the fortified walls of Constantinople. Simple gunpowder delivered payloads obliterated the walls. I was one of the first to enter by making my way over a pile of rubble which now spilled into one of the outer streets of the besieged city. The first person I was aware of was a woman dressed in long black chador. Her eyes were visible through an opening between the lower face and forehead. Something compelled me to approach her. I felt she was drawing me toward her. And she stood her ground staring at me as I drew closer. There was something in her eyes, a magnetism that grew stronger as I got closer. There was a wild kind of power in her eyes. I heard an interior voice, whispering, feminine, commanding, telling me to bring my

sword down on her neck. She dropped after I struck and her head rolled around me, as if animated by a will, describing a full circle. I stood there for an incalculable time, looking down into the dead but alive eyes staring up from the head which was now floating in a shallow puddle of blood. There was a mixture of rage and pain in her eyes, but not a trace of fear. I blinked and was lost in darkness.

Ultra level #2 was a brief science fiction film title PLECTURS PARVUS. It opened with the extraction of Permafrost from a layer in Northeastern Siberia in the mid 21st Century. Ancient history. It was staged with the sobriety of a science documentary. A team of scientists in white parkas dug the sample out and deposited in a portable freezer which was delivered post haste to a secret laboratory near Moscow. The camera followed the movements of a scientist as a slide was placed in a microscopic chamber. "It's a 42 thousand year old nematode" the young woman in a white lab coat narrated into an overhead microphone. "It is highly radioactive for something its size but not dangerous to humans." Her voice faltered as she fell to the floor, jerking wildly as she endured what would become 48 hours of non-stop hallucinations. In the first hallucination she experienced projection into an area inside the nematode. It was like being in a huge reddish sack with sticky surfaces and a pungent citrus odor. Then she heard the voice, it spoke in high pitched, dulcet tones, "You are within the power and everything will become revealed." She later told debriefing that she had the certitude that she was in contact with an unknown, very powerful, secret gnosis, an unknown and unknowable religion capable of world domination.

I was physically and emotionally exhausted by the immersion in the Ultras. I somehow now had the certainty that Simone was indeed dead, not just disappeared. I wanted to leave the clinic as soon as possible. But I had to speak with Doctor Chavanne first. Francis Chavanne was born in Paris and studied psychiatry there. He spoke nine languages perfectly, and there was only a faint hint of a French accent in his elegant English. "You have a heightened state of interest which approaches obsession," was the first things he said to me in his office, which was a multi dimensional platform of screens and stages bubbling with colorful holograms and projections. "Human nature in all its finery,' I quipped back, not smiling. "I'm presently stripped of the vanity of human wishes. I hope I will be able to interrogate an arcane aspect of human nature before I expire." He rose and peered into a hologram of the teeming hive which was Istanbul. "I sense your coach awaits somewhere above," he said as if it were an inside joke. "Or is your destination Mount Etna?" A ceiling screen showed lava roiling within Etna's crater which segued into footage from a mid-20th Century film depicting the destruction of Pompeii by the volcano. Citizens of the city were shown being crushed by falling architecture, running for cover and being burned alive by magma. I had the sudden certainty Chavannes was a hologram which was designed only for my benefit. And then there was a fade to black.

Ultra level #3: The Conditioning Room was identified by a psi projected plaque. I was being prepared for the Istanbul run. Audio-video input: I heard Simone's voice in my mind; it spoke with slow certitude, "My god will punish you." The tone was unsettling, as if it came from a powerful, knowing source. That wasn't Simone, she had a tendency to be ambiguous, qualifying ev-

erything, and tended to speak in quick-fire whispers.. But, who is this god? My attention was dominated by a new holographic scene. The room had become a vividly detailed set of a mosque in Istanbul. I was outside the mosque at first, looking up at a spire. A young blonde woman in a black leather jump suit walked up to me very quickly and pointed to a figure in the door of the mosque. "Mr. Hitchcock wants to speak with you… now, please!"

I was quickly briefed by a thought implant that Alfred Hitchcock, who had died nearly 100 years ago, was directing a spy thriller set in Istanbul. I was greeted by a free floating, demonstration hologram of the director at the mosque's main entrance. "Listen!" Hitchcock commanded quietly and rather politely. "Now if you will just walk in, stop at the fountain in the reception area, the actress will walk in, pull out a gun and fire. It will all be done in one take so you don't have to fall. We'll be cutting to a flash of red. If you do nothing more than walk in, stop, and look at the actress the scene will work." I wanted to say, like you did in SPELLBOUND, but I held my tongue. He smiled as if he knew what I was thinking. Hitchcock suddenly dissolved as holograms sometimes do. I was already in the room with the fountain. Simone, who was dressed in a shocking white chador, came out from an interior room, approached me quickly, pulled out a gun, and fired a silent shot toward my stomach. I saw the red flash, as Hitchcock described, just as I closed my eyes quickly. There was some traditional Turkish music, a song performed by a female vocalist, emanating from another room in the Istanbul set. Simone's voice warned, "The threat is from inner space…"

I remind myself that I am a spy in

an Alfred Hitchcock scenario. Everything is now in the present tense. And like one of those adventures, nothing was real, and like a good suspense screenplay everything is suddenly happening in the anxious now. I have the feeling that Simone must have taken her life while on assignment. Suicide was always an option with her. I hear her voice again. "I'm calling the shots!" That's all I could make out. Then the scene unfolds between her and a striking actress playing the role of the goddess Kali. The room is doing what it needs to do. Kali is wrapped in South Asian garments. A matching magenta Dupatta and long flowing dress. A smile lights her face but the color of the clothing seems to roll my mood toward a weighted depression. Kali's psi powers are far superior to Simone's.

The scene continues as staged theatrical event with a projected image of mosque in Istanbul as a backdrop.

Simone: "I want to move toward Istanbul... I have a meeting with Alfred Hitchcoc

Kali (tenderly) "I'm not blocking you, I'm here to guide you."

Simone: "Why are you named after the goddess of death and violence?"

Kali: "Kali is also Parvati, the goddess of love and happiness. Death is the gateway to renewal and a state of continuous ecstasy."

Simone: "I want to experience revelation.."

Kali: "You will, if you meditate on the hour every day. You will, if you stay healthy by cleansing your system of all but water. You will, if you learn to laugh at yourself. You will, if you overcome your fear of the unknowable. " Remember, I am not doomsday, death, eternal blackness, my dear. You are...."

Both women turn toward the projection which becomes black and white documentary style film showing an ancient multi-cellular organism moving slowly the a shallow river of mud. It was impossible to judge the scale of the event. The creature fills the narrow tunnel it progresses through as it bears down on a lump of biomass which will be its nourishment for the present moment. I have the feeling that I am auditing a film within a film which is a recording of an ancient event. What was it? Where is it happening? I have the unsettling experience of being an invisible camera recording a play.

Simone: (turning toward the camera): "I'll tell you where I'm going if you promise to meet me there."

I watched the scene, as if I were suspended in space, or a fly positioned high on the wall of consciousness. Then I realized I was at the end of this Ultra.

Ultra level #4: It is 4 Billion BCE. The object bears down toward Earth at great velocity. It is an incalculably hot mass around a center constructed specifically for the Zed .9, a mass containing a toxic mixture carbon monoxide and methane which surrounds a capsule in which the X lives. I have been projected into the front of the mass so I am experiencing the vector first hand, front and center. Finally, just before entering the atmosphere, I black out. I come to consciousness within the capsule; I am surrounded by what appears to be an organic sac. I hear chanting voices around me and a cinema-like dissolve reveals that I am

in a green chambe[...] by
figures wearing lo[...] robes and
hoods. Mind racing [...] sentenc-
es are difficult. I [...] at the head
of the entity borin[...] through the
substratum now. My head crashes
through rock, mud, deep roots. There
is no oxygen above the surface but
down here that doesn't matter. Pre-
exi[...]ent life forms and the magnet-
ic [...]aves from the far [...]ure play
aro[...]nd me. Voices, some of them familiar surround me, talking about
a terrible rain falling. A terrible
rain is falling on the surface. But
a terrible rain has been falling
for as long as I have been conscious. A stern voice threatens to
[...]ve me burned at the sta[...], in public durin[...] a future medieval trial as I have been condemned as a
Templar. It all seems to be slowing
down now. You are very disturbed,
another voice, female, whispers gently. The voices blur together. There
are screeching sounds, animal like
calls, and then the sounds of water flushing out of the capsule.
I make sure I have my breathing
equipment ready since a change of
environment is imminent.

Ultra level #5: I emerge from a
thick mud onto the shore of Istanbul in the mid [...]th Century. A
large cargo airplane flew low
overhead. The sound of its engines
is deafening. At the same time I realize that I have not left the clinic and likely never will. I'm aware
of that, but not who is in control,
although I have my suspicions.
Istanbul is an imposing cyclorama
which stretches across my field of
vision. The Battle for Constantinople was fought centuries ago and
there's little evidence of it left.
In fact, it's been completely washed
out of the screen. In see a land
rover moving toward my position.
The driver, a young Turkish woman,
smiles as I take my seat. "I hope
you had a good trip," is her greet-
ing and I immediately realize she's
[...] Synthetic. "It was interesting,"

I reply out of useless courtesy.
"I'm taking you right to Mr. Hitchcock," she informs me reassuring me.
"Yes, I thought so." We pull up in
front of a gold plated mosque as
my meeting with Alfred Hitchcock
is about to be replayed. I expect
an assistant to emerge but Hitchcock himself slowly walks toward
me, patting his sweating forehead
with a red handkerchief. "Welcome,
and lunch it waiting," he motions
toward a white tiled reception area
within. I marvel at the holographic
technique used in creating Hitchcock. He's perfectly well mannered
and at the same time self depre-
cating. And I imagine his taste in
wine and food will be exquisite.

"You see, or you think you see,"
Hitch said with a childish grin.
"But I'm making a new kind of experience here; an experimental
reality in which I will make available entertainment and artistic
design." Hitchcock frowns, and then
smiles, but with Hitch a smile is
just an upside down frown. Even
in his carefully engineered hologram state he presents a series of
personal and professional quirks.
Pointing up at the spiraling gold
gilded staircase which snakes its
way to the top of the mosque Hitchcock is suddenly in command mode.
Or shall we say suggestion. This
Hitchcock is a director in name
and order number only. He seems to
suggest, when he intends to have
commands promptly executed. "You
follow her up the staircase…. slowly, very deliberately. You won't
see her, but she'll be in the scene.
We'll put her in later." I silently
thought the he had already made
this film, if not in actuality, then
in his mind. But it was all a holographic experience in a cyclorama…. Nothing is real. I can't even
be sure of what state of consciousness I have entered. I am a spy in a
Hitchcock suspense thriller, that's
all I know at the moment. The last
thing I remember is that the image

of Hitchcock withdrew; he was a perfect free-floating hologram.

Simone's voice, whispering, "Take the tunnel to the minaret, ascend to the top. Follow the blond actress..." I am in the blackness of the tunnel moving toward the unknown. My encounter with Hitchcock was over. I feel compelled to play a role in a film which didn't have to be recorded with cameras. They didn't exist anymore. Only Ultras exist now. Some are short; some are long. Each Ultra leads me to another level. For one second before the transition I was back in the Upstate New York clinic where everything was frozen in a midwinter ice sculpture. Then I realize that I've been there all along....

Ultra level #6: I am in the base of the minaret. If I look through the port at eye level I can see the mosque and an expanse of the Istanbul cyclorama. The unreality is overwhelmingly real. I am stuck in a perpetual present tense conundrum where the object of my search is out of reach and probably wants me dead, or at least completely forgotten. There's no pleasure for me in this Hitchcock film. It's not even a film which one can relax and enjoy. It's an incomprehensible spiral into the wishes of forces more powerful than my thoughts. My conscious mind is buffeted with images of a massive snake or woman with a human head which is pursuing me as I ascend toward the top of the minaret. Then there are thousands of racing still and moving images, all printed in negative format. Tightly packed crowds of thuggish, Spanish conquistadors in heavy metal protection, mounds of starved, dead bodies in the 20th Century Nazi death camps, weakened ruffled shirted aristocrats being shuffled quickly toward towering guillotines in 18th Century France, piles of slaughtered Native Americans being examined by Union Cavalry for valuables and scalps, German, French, American soldiers, freezing and frightened in World War I European trenchers, lines of mounted soldiers racing toward the wall of a medieval city with sharp swords in one hand, stirrups in the other.

I catch a glimpse of Hitchcock's elusive blond on the flight above me. She disappears into the tower room. A moment later I look to the left portal and see her body rapidly falling out of view. Where had I seen this all before? I rushed up to the tower room, pushing open a heavy wooden door to enter. The room is a bare elliptical space with one barred window. An elliptical black marble table is in the center. The head of mountain goat lies in a pool of blood in the center of the table. Simone, wearing a golden robe and flanked by 12 female bishops, six on each side of her, is holding a bloody axe aloft. For an indeterminate time I am frozen in place, as are the coven. I am certain that they are a coven of intellectuals, rather than witches; that they have read libraries of which I have never been aware. I have the compulsion to move downward, toward the underworld. All will be revealed in the underworld, the voice of Kali is whispering, "Hell is not at the center of the Earth..." That geographic hell is now in sight, despite its conceptual distance. The path was littered with false entrances and exits. My task was to ignore them and move forward. Not as easy as it sounds. Hitchcock suddenly appears in a grotto off the main path. The grotto is illuminated with an icy blue light and Hitchcock is seated in a director's chair at a black ivory table with two small espresso cups on each side. "Come and have a cup of espresso; we have to talk." He sounds friendly, inviting but I have my doubts.

Hitch leans toward me, "The name of the film is Detour into Hell." He leans back and smiles. Sharing a small space with a hologram is always unsettling, but having seen all of the films of the 20th Century auteur who was considered one of the greatest artists to work in cinema, whose films had been fetishes, analyzed, remade, and been cultural icons, was more than unsettling, it was frightening. What made him tick? I wonder as I await his follow-up. "There's been the mystery blond female whom you pursue through Istanbul. Your motives are sexual. But she's actually a double agent, planted to blackmail you, to get at the whatever-it-is." I feel as if I'm missing something. "What do the intruders want?" I ask impertinently. Hitch is visibly taken aback. Finally he says, "I'm going to show you."

"Astral projection," Hitchcock says, loudly, clearly, as if it were an order. Suddenly the grotto is filled with the presence of a huge nematode with a human head. The head looks familiar but I can't quite place the face." Hitch was projecting his internal self into physical space. "Pyrokinesis," he then quips and the creature is immediately immolated by an arc of fire which disappears as quickly as it appeared. "Those are just two," Hitchcock smiles as he holds up two fingers." Hitch was the most entertaining hologram I had even experienced. He was witty, unpredictable and memorable, like his creations. You didn't want to leave his presence. But there was an undercurrent of insincerity about him, maybe engineered in as a kind of warning that he was not to be taken seriously even if one wanted to take him very seriously indeed. He was like a good magician who excelled at the art of distraction.

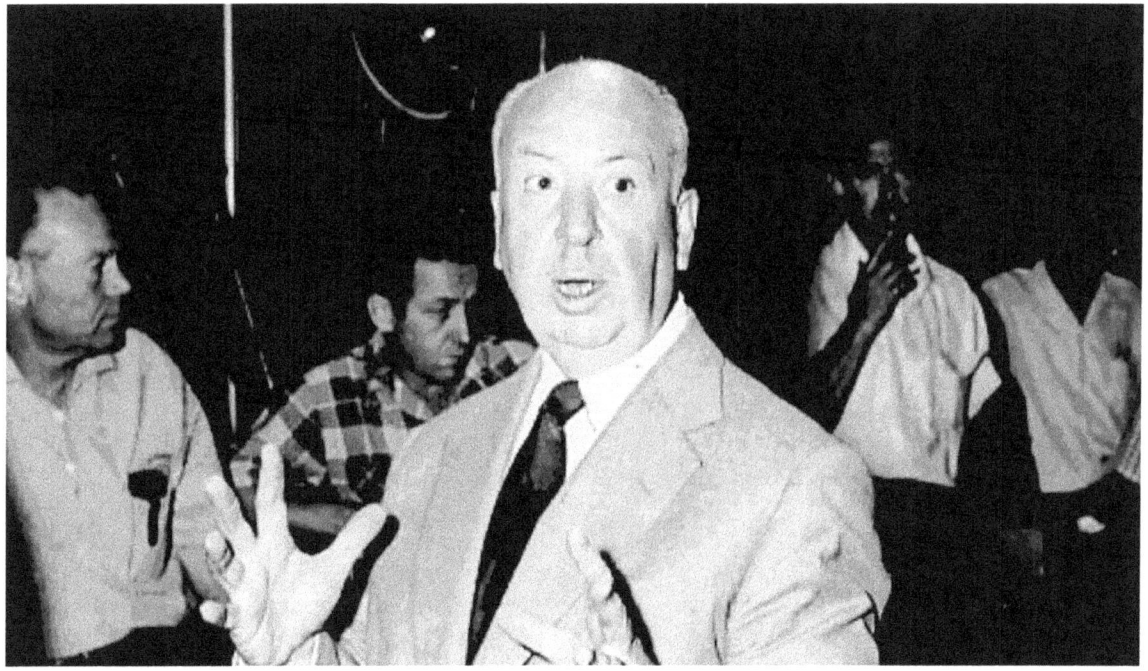

Ultra level #7: Hitch's final act in the grotto was to use the Game's Reality Conjuration function on me. I will narrate the rest using Retro cognition and the past tense. Back on the downward spiral I was aware of a subtle change in the climate. Specifically, it got colder and a wind was buffeting me. I wasn't sure if it was an unknown supernatural force or some kind of energy manipulation radiating from the unconscious of Simone. I didn't hear her voice but the words Reim Kennars, written in white paint on the tunnel wall, greeted me at the next turn. Was it a cult in which she was a member? Murmuring voices were chanting the words and I was suddenly certain that they held power in this realm.

I started to see a large eagle's head swirling above me, which slowly morphed into a decapitated human head covered with long white hair and which had a black veil over its face. A film takes place in the present tense, like life, but this report will from here on will confine itself to the past. The Reim Kennars inhabit a past that is literary (Sir Walter Scott) and expanded into my journey toward the buried truth. And the trust is always buried. Only lies and sex are on the surface. A liquid fade into another past brought me to the Carnival at Izmid. At the center of the area was a Dolmen, a prehistoric, megalithic structure formed by a huge flat stone laid across other large stones place upright. A faint crimson glow was visible within the structure. An agent has to accept assignments and carry them out. When an agent starts asking too many questions about the assignments failure became more likely. The wind seemed to have a supernatural force behind it. Or was it just a trick of my mind? Or was it all being projected into my consciousness by a cult, or a science authority?

They emerged out of the glow. They were dressed in bloody animal skins. Simone was at the center of the group wearing a white goat's skin. Her face was wrinkled with age and her eyes tiny black indentations.

The Reim Kennars chanted quietly at first, and then the volume rose to a level which made my ears ring:

"Sun is our life, Moon is our life…. Sun is our life, Moon is our life…" over and over. It was ridiculous at first, but in time became hypnotic.

Then Simone spoke, slowly, quietly, "Just before midnight…. I walked across Izmid. I knew that this would be the last night. The end of a cycle. I saw what others had seen. I saw life in Santorini, Atlantis, and Magog… I saw life in ancient Babylon, Crete, and Byzantium. All while the Reim Kennars waited. The mound builders waited. The city of Uruk waited. We are the Reim Kennars and will not wait another thousand years….we have come to take the planet." Then she stepped aside and the image of Kali appeared, swathed in golden garments. She said, quoting William Blake's THE FIRST BOOK OF URIZEN, "Of the primeval priest's assumed powers… When eternals spurned back his religion and gave him a place in the North, obscure, shadowy, void solitary. "

The velocity of the demon wind picked up considerably. There was a palpable taste of bitter lemon in the wind and it seemed to now have a deep magenta color. Human eyes and scattered voices could be seen and heard as the gusts got more violent. Wind can tear a human apart at specific velocities and this one seemed capable of freezing a person to death. I had the revelation that this was a wind which had blown through history and had powers to kill or to spontaneously create life forms. The history of all religions was in this wind. The Game was reaching some kind of crescendo….

Ultra level # 8: The words King Crab flashed in the distance, indicating a portal entrance. The demon wind was powering down. It was a mind-fuck all along. Inside the King Crab portal a pink hued hell decorated with silver painted sex workers greeted my tired eyes. Several of the sensual workers interacted with oversized, brown skinned crustaceans. hence, King Crab. I wished I were like the Hitch hologram, whose eyes never faltered and who would live forever. I was so far beneath Istanbul that the reality above, conventional space and time, didn't matter anymore. Hell is where nothing matters anymore. It didn't matter if she were the High Priestess of Pangea or a former friend or an assignment. There was one more level below. A game offi-cer wearing crustacean body armor came over to the table and leaned toward me, whispering "Tracer, you're going down."

Ultra level #9: It was in an area of complete darkness. I couldn't move forward or backward. Suddenly an arc light illuminated fi gures in hooded robes. Simone was at the cen-ter of the group. Then she stepped aside to reveal Kali, still swathed in golden garments. She held a de-capitated head high with her right hand. It took me about a minute to recognize the head was my own. By the time you read this I will be recycled. Simone no longer existed. There were no Reim Kennars. There were no mythologies, legends, or dreams to explore. I was a Tracer with nothing to trace. Nonetheless the image of the goddess Kali stood there holding my severed head and staring into my eyes with a trium-phant smile on her lips. It was a coup-de-theater I had dreaded, but on one level expected. The Game was over. My report will be fi led post haste and nothing will be revealed. I was in the land of the dead. I had been dead a long time. But I was granted a reprieve under cer-tain conditions. I was 100 human and not down for the count, but I was hoping for alt-cyborg consid-eration. But I ignored those con-ditions, being more interested in playing the contact game of life. Communication with the dead is al-ways a dangerous business.

A CELEBRATED WRITER AND FILMMAKER, ROBERT MONELL IS ONE OF THE LEADING AUTHORITIES ON EUROPEAN GENRE CINEMA IN THE WORLD.

HIS WORK HAS APPEARED IN A VARIETY OF ACCLAIMED BOOKS, JOURNALS, MAGAZINES AND WEBSITES INCLUDING THE LANDMARK BLOG HE CREATED, I'M IN A JESS FRANCO STATE OF MIND.

HE IS ALSO AN ADMINSTRATOR AT THE POPULAR FILM FORUM CINEMADROME.

FOLLOW HIM AT

INSTAGRAM.COM/ROBERTMONELL/

FACEBOOK.COM/ROBERT.MONELL

AND

TWITTER.COM/BOBM579

The font used for Robert's story is called Traveling Typewriter. It was made in West Germany by Carl Krull from an old Danish "Olympia Traveler de luxe" typewriter. Any inconsistencies found in the font are deliberate and part of its charm.

P
RORY
DEMAIO
T
R
Y

5 NEW POEMS
BY
RORY DEMAIO

apart we're quite

apart i'm quite
a different thing.

without the weight
of your arms
to center my toss-turn tenden-
cies,
i place four fingers
to stake out my breast bone
counting hard edges
to press,test
something solid.

i roll over
to let my head slosh around
with all the memories so soft
and unformed within that
tissue
where they live
with the pliable possibility
of   shift.

but am i right in thinking
too much cushion
is too much pressure?
since that can lead
to any number of fractures

i've only watched other people
packing up boxes and
stuffing in feelings-
rigid or loose,
no example to go by

maybe that's better.

well,
if maybe is better,
maybe i'll let my fingers fall
to your side
(the cool space on the bed)
my brain gummy
in a weird-hopeful way.

me, too.

the longest strand i held too dear
lay in my arm
crooked and narrow.

sometimes i'd pull it out
and hold it to the light
where we could see if it matched other ends
with dripping dyes
or sun swallowed pastels,
but every night,
i'd tuck it back
trying to rethread its pattern in my dreams.

you'd see pieces strung up,
looped together,
stitched brightly on breast pockets,
and even some neatly lined on banquet tables

and still here, me,
my thread,
hands clammy
and whispery nags about
fault and imperfections ,
nightly faded starts and chases.

so when ghost stories grew to unspoiled heights,
i shivered
and tossed the strand so steeped
that it soared,
smacked
the gravel, spitting
those few last words, wet
and hot

the last boiled bits of a tired trauma.

millennial

when the current glint has been cocoa dusted
and the week begins
to graph itself,
searing
the slick back of my eyes,
i focus

here
on the husky sheen of improperly inked details
that overlap in the space
                              (of us)

though fragmented and
shooed about
with nibbling bits of lists and hows and justs,
i can weigh down some lashes
and slow even some rise
to vibrate in now
with yet
            over
                        under

folded in with your cracked pepper grin
and a pickup-sticks halo,
you're an icon molded in sheets
so

I quickly trace those lids
feeling for a dream-soft wool
but nothing
just blue
yours seeing mine

this, a whole
soft and muted,
warm in a hard-won us-ness

and then a slice of a screen
(all it takes)
and my paper-stored thoughts
sputter
til all the blues are gone
leaving only hot afterimages

peeking/peaking

not too far back,
i had a pocket
of air
that i massaged, waved
a silent hello
with my hand to my sternum
a bright bubble beneath
waiting for Then.

I felt sure.
it was there; I was, too.
I knew what hurt
and that I was strong.
I had an aura.
(though, god, I wouldn't call it an aura)
it followed Me
sweet and thick,
basking in the knowledge (I knew!)
that it would lead
and I could follow.

but,
here—
i'm fogged, breathing shallow
or sighing?
a great steam all over my mirror
and simple, studied,
majestically subdued grief
soaks my shape

it's not who I was
a brash streak of righteousness
because i let it go,
never mapped it out,
let a persona get tumble-torn
and too heavy

i thought it was just coming
it would be charged with all could,
exuded, knew, was
a few more memories and then fall into rhythm

yet I followed should, sorry,
                              but,
perfecting an anxious glaze so sharp
the reflection was blindingly white.

so here we are.
stuck with just the tapping,
checking cracks and smoothing over
as each next one appears.

so i'll admit it. i need her back.
she knew Me.
and I am her.
We are Then.
and this has to be now.

us

on the day
and in the days that followed
we picked and flecked the snow
shivered, remembering
we never heard it falling.

there's a question
 and more,
a deliberate pulling of why,
how so many separate sorrows
came to lie down,
packing walls hard and fast.

for those
they have portioned time and heavy ownership to the other
too much is wrong and right is righteous.
pinned proudly to their fluorescent baked cork,
their solutions that blanket nooks and crannies
and their guilt-driven dreams chant reminders
all just papers they leave
to cycle through the next pixelated spiral
of weight at home

and those
hidden behind the white mounds beside
they wonder,
wonder what weathered hands can texture next
because they belong to so many--
and they wonder why no one takes notice
because they don't like to do the talking
(well now that you're riled up)
not even the reading
just pressing against eyelids
pulsing whatahellofaday whatisthisnow
or sampling the bread before it hits the table

and all to think
oh how so many chests can crack at once
scarlet and blued,
spitting dust ,

the sooty remains of silent cuts.

it's not even everyone.
just most
and some.
but the flakes had hardened
and they had to pick sides.

so we swept.
and we gathered our boots
to trace the room
in an uneasy anonymity of shades.

here, with slow-eared hums
and chapped pink lungs
we rasped a lullaby
only the notes didn't put down heads
merely found more sound

so,
far down the lane
into a two-tone house
where a quilt is being stitched
(slow)
pierced
and stiffly linked
the sticky music tinkles
and there
a gathered stack
of fabric aided stories
lengthens
warming knees,
bruised
and creaking

I was born and raised in Louisville and Lexington, Kentucky, but I gathered a good bit of spice from living in New Orleans for six years. I studied Art History in undergrad and grad school at Tulane University, because I feel the necessity of memory, lesson, inspiration, and aspiration for humanity and beauty. I can't seem to nail down a singular creative passion, dabbling in multiple media, but writing has always been my constant. I treat words preciously. My childhood "journals" were compilations of song lyrics and novel phrases that ignited a clear picture or lists of beloved words like a meditative chant of similar sounds. Every word has a clear taste, texture, or hue in my mind; I often start a piece by choosing one word or a phrase that feels appropriate for a situation and expand from there. These strong aesthetic contexts allow for me to give an image to abstracts and emotions that feel so illusive in reality.
You can follow me at Instagram @rorydemaio

-Rory Demaio-

LOU·REED

Available on Cassette,
LP and Compact Disc
From

SIRE

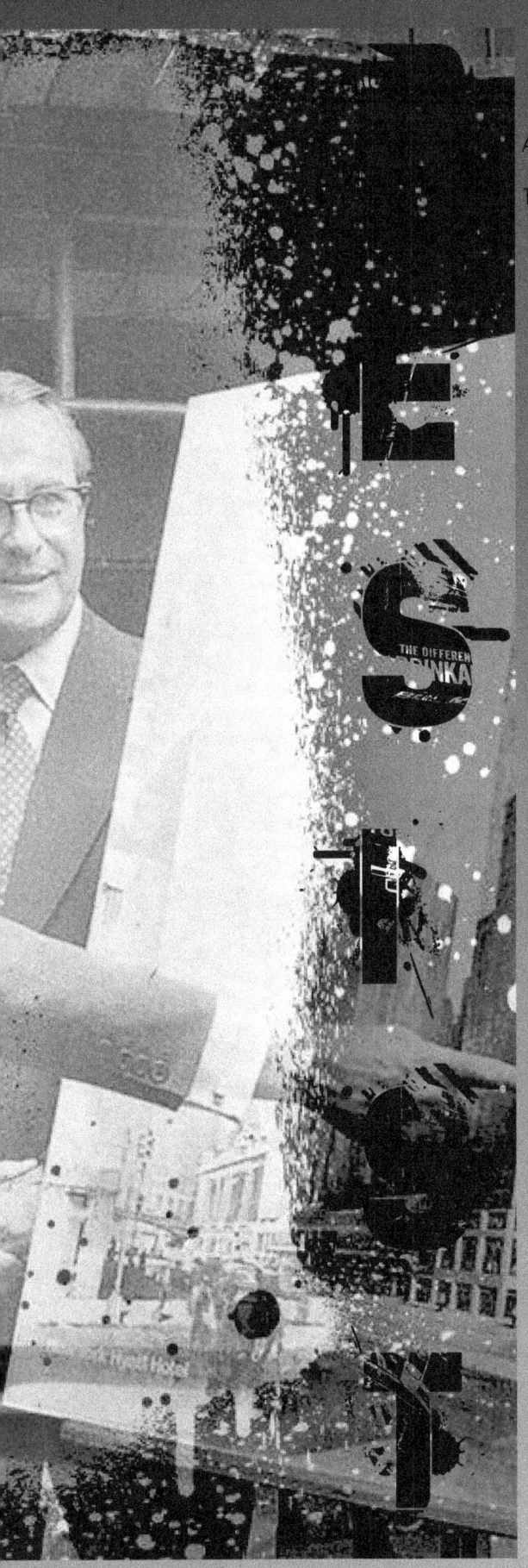

SICK OF YOU

"I was up in the morning with the TV blarin'
brush my teeth sittin' watchin' the news
All the beaches were closed the ocean was a Red Sea
but there was no one there to part it in two
There was no fresh salad because there's hypos in the
cabbage
Staten Island disappeared at noon
And they say the midwest is in great distress
and NASA blew up the moon
The ozone layer has no ozone anymore
and you're gonna leave me for the guy next door
I'm Sick of You
They arrested the Mayor for an illegal favor
sold the Empire State to Japan
And Oliver North married William Secord
and gave birth to a little Teheran
And the Ayatollah bought a nuclear warhead
if he dies he wants to go out in style
And there's nothing to eat that don't carry the stink
of some human waste dumped in the Nile
Well one thing is certainly true
no one here knows what to do
I'm Sick of You
The radio said there were 400 dead
in some small town in Arkansas
Some whacked out trucker
drove into a nuclear reactor
and killed everybody he saw
Now he's on Morton Downey
and he's glowing and shining
doctors say this is a medical advance
They say the bad makes the good
and there's something to be learned
in every human experience
Well I know one thing that really is true
This here's a zoo and the keeper ain't you
And I'm sick of it, I'm Sick of You
They ordained the Trumps
and then he got the mumps
and died being treated at Mt. Sinai
And my best friend Bill
died from a poison pill
some wired doctor prescribed for stress
My arms and legs are shrunk
the food all has lumps
They discovered some animal no one's ever seen
It was an inside trader eating a rubber tire
after running over Rudy Giuliani
They say the President's dead
but no one can find his head
It's been missing now for weeks
But no one noticed it
he has seemed so fit
and I'm Sick of it."

-LOU REED, 1989-

"Weeping, weeping, weeping.
We created cars to
fight for space to be in.
We created w... ...
waste our time.
We created love
so one can
be the victim.
We all need love,
but don't know what to do
with it...
I don't want to carry on
Except I can't even
cease to exist.
And that's the worst."